THIS BOOK IS WRITTEN FOR OUR KIDS:

James & Samuel, Nic,
Maya & Beth, Luke & Jess.
We hope to open the doors
of YOUR imagination, to the
wonder of AFRICA!

© Publication: Penguin Random House South Africa (Pty) Ltd,
The Estuaries No 4, Oxbow Crescent, Century Avenue, Century City, 7441
PO Box 1144, Cape Town, 8000
www.penguinrandomhouse.co.za

© Text: Riaan Manser & Murray Williams
Cover design: Renthia Buitendag

Publisher: Nandi Lessing-Venter
Edited by: Murray Williams & Chantal Tarling
Proofread by: Glenda Laity

Design and layout by Renthia Buitendag — Stickart
Set in 14.5 pt on 21 pt GeoSans Light

Gedruk deur **novus print**, 'n afdeling van Novus Holdings

First edition 2022
Second impression 2022
Third impression 2022

ISBN 978 1 7763 5372 9 (printed book)
ISBN 978 1 7763 5373 6 (ePub)

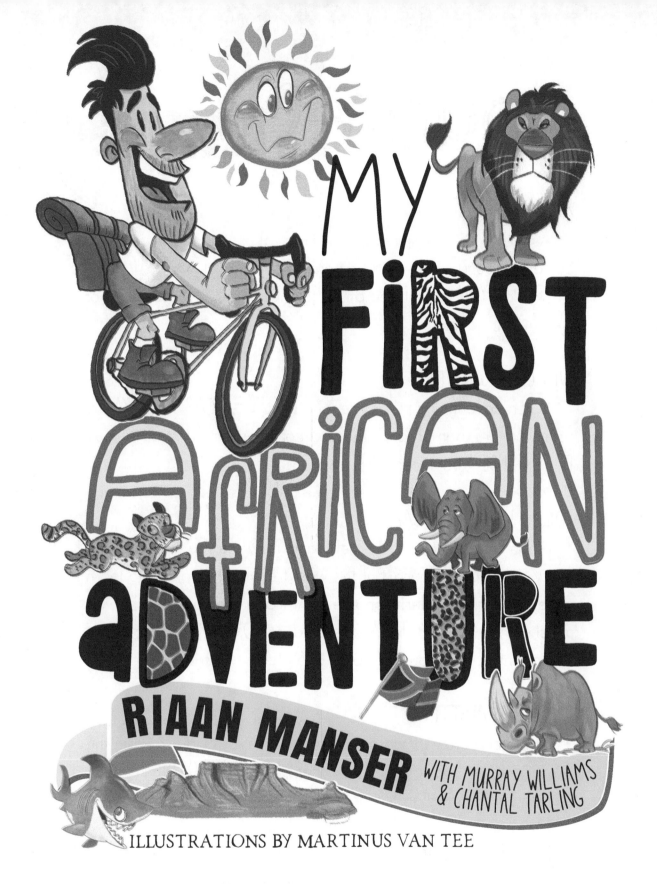

MY FIRST AFRICAN ADVENTURE

RIAAN MANSER
WITH MURRAY WILLIAMS & CHANTAL TARLING

ILLUSTRATIONS BY MARTINUS VAN TEE

STRUIK CHILDREN

www.penguinrandomhouse.co.za

QUOTES

MAMA AFRICA!

❝ As a child, I was inspired by this magical continent of Africa. So, as a young man, I was determined to see it with MY OWN EYES! Now YOU can join me on my journey, through these pages of AWESOME adventure! ❞

WHY CYCLING IS BEST:

❝ When adventuring by bicycle, one can SEE, HEAR AND SMELL so much more than on any other form of transport. Try it out – you'll EXPERIENCE what I mean! ❞

BOY, DO I LOVE AFRICA:

❝ I soon learned how to say 'Hello' and 'How are you' in Swahili and every language in Africa. But this wasn't enough! I wanted to learn more about the wonderful people of Africa, in every country! SO: Let me share the FUN FACTS I've learned, so YOU can ALSO become friends with the wonderful people and places of Africa too! ❞

EVERY DAY MATTERS:

❝ At the end of every day on my adventure, I would try watch the Sunset and say 'Goodnight' to another day of EXPLORING in Africa. I remember being so grateful to be healthy and alive! WOW! ❞

THE POWER OF SONG:

❝ It's amazing to see how music can unite people from totally different worlds! ❞

ALWAYS FACE EAST:

❝ There's a mountain peak, the HIGHEST POINT in Africa, from which you can see the sun rise over the whole continent! At 07h30 on July 3, 2005, I reached the summit of Mount Kilimanjaro, the mighty Uhuru Peak, and I saw Africa stretched out before me – north, south, east & west. NOW that I've seen Africa from the highest point, we can go EXPLORE Africa together... LET'S GO! ❞

SCAN here for more sights and sounds of Rigan's adventure around Africa!

29 SOMALIA
28 DJIBOUTI
27 ERITREA
30 ETHIOPIA
31 KENYA
32 TANZANIA
26 SUDAN
25 EGYPT
24 LIBYA
23 TUNISIA
TIP OF AFRICA
HALF WAY
22 ALGERIA
21 MOROCCO
20 SAHARA
19 MAURITANIA
18 THE GAMBIA
17 SENEGAL
16 GUINEA-BISSAU
15 GUINEA
14 SIERRA LEONE
13 LIBERIA
12 IVORY COAST
11 GHANA
10 TOGO
9 BENIN
8 NIGERIA
7 CAMEROON
6 EQUATORIAL GUINEA
5 GABON
4 THE REPUBLIC OF THE CONGO
3 DEMOCRATIC REPUBLIC OF THE CONGO

InDex

NAMIBIA

LANGUAGES: English, Oshiwambo, Khoekhoe, Afrikaans, Herero, Kwangali, German, Portuguese and others.

CAPITAL: Windhoek

POPULATION: 2,618,733

CURRENCY: Namibian Dollar

FLAG:

ADVENTURE ATTRACTIONS:
Kolmanskop's 'ghost town',
an abandoned diamond-mining town;
view wildlife in the Etosha National Park;
canoe and hike in the Fish River Canyon.

FABULOUS FOOD:
OMAGUNGU
Mopane worms, fried until crispy.

NATIONAL ANIMAL:
GEMSBOK
An antelope also known as the ORYX.

SPEAK:
'Good morning, are you doing well?'
OSHIWAMBO:
'Mwa lala po, owu li nawa?'

BORDER

KEETMANSHOOP

WINDHOEK

AFRICA, HERE I COME!

I was ready for Africa... but was Africa ready for ME?

I'd left South Africa and crossed into Namibia, pedalling up long, dusty roads through kudu country. IT WAS HOT, HOT, HOT!

The heat rose in clouds off the tar – like waves of lava off a volcano.

Or sticking your head in an oven.

Every time a huge truck thundered past, it pulled along a cloud of air behind it.

I did my best to catch their slipstreams – like catching a free ride in a moving bubble!

I soon fell into a night-time camping routine. I knew I needed to look after myself, since I was the bike's 'engine', so I had to get enough sleep and eat super-healthily. I wondered what crazy new types of foods I'd find on my journey!

But sometimes it was difficult to find a place to sleep, because Namibia feels like one big game park. One night, I pitched my tent next to the highway,

between two thick thorn trees. As dusk fell, some magnificent kudu bulls were silhouetted against the flaming orange of the setting sun. I fell asleep quietly, with this beautiful picture in my mind.

Suddenly, I was pulled out of my peaceful sleep by the thud-thud sound of many hooves running together, towards me. STAMPEDE!

The herd of huge kudus was charging towards my campsite, panicked by something. One was coming right for me... a 400kg beast.

THANK GOODNESS FOR THE THORN TREES! The kudu split perfectly around my tent, wedged between my wonderful two 'guards' – the thorn trees.

You may think the Big Five are the most dangerous animals in our wild and untamed Africa, but these enormous antelopes are just as fearsome, with their sharp horns, like pairs of swords. I'd have to be careful of a whole lot more animals than I thought...

TSUMEB   ONDANGWA

FLAG:

CAPITAL: Luanda

ANGOLA

NATIONAL ANIMAL: Giant Sable Antelope

POPULATION: 34,645,375

SPEAK:
'Good morning, how are you?'
UMBUNDU:
'Wosala ndati, wakala-po ciwo?'

LANGUAGES:
Portuguese (official language), Umbundu, Kimbundu, Kikongo, Chokwe, Kwanyama (Oshikwanyama), Ngangela, French and English and others.

FAMOUS PERSON:
ARTUR CARLOS MAURICIO PESTANA DOS SANTOS
a major novelist who writes under the name Pepetela.

ADVENTURE ATTRACTIONS:
Kalandula Waterfalls, one of the biggest waterfalls by volume in Africa;
Tundavala Volcanic Fissure, a spectacular viewpoint;
Bicuar National Park to view elephant, buffalo, cheetah and leopard.

FABULOUS FOOD: MUFETE
A dish made from grilled fish, beans, onions, plantains, sweet potato and cassava.

BORDER

BENGUELA

LUANDA

INTO THE LAND OF DIAMONDS AND TSETSES!

Angola started off flat and open, but the dry veld soon changed to bush, dotted with baobab trees. Baobab trees look very beautiful and strange, almost like upside-down trees, with up-facing roots, like wild, waving arms!

It was boiling hot as I started to make my way over 16 very long, steep hills to the jungle city of Lubango.

My friend, Frank, had given me some advice: 'Make sure that you go downhill really, really fast, because it'll help carry you up the next hill,' he said. IT WORKED!

When I arrived in Lubango, I couldn't find anywhere to sleep. I knocked on lots of doors, but still no luck...

Finally, a family saw me, freezing cold and out on the street, and let me into their little home. I fell asleep gratefully. But when I woke the next morning, there was an old man curled up on the floor of my bedroom. I'd been sleeping in his bed! That's what you call extreme hospitality. ⟶ I felt terrible!

I cycled on towards the sea, past a tiny village of five huts, with their own home-grown energy bars: sugar cane. I've never eaten so much sugar in my life and I was like a kid after too many sweets at a birthday party. Bouncing off the walls!

They were even more excited when I set up my tent in the place of honour – next to the headman's hut. → **I felt like an African prince!**

The next morning, pedalling out of the village and into the rising sun, I wondered if they'd tell their children the story of the Strange Bearded Bicycle Man! I'll remember them forever because they had such kind hearts.

Next, I was cycling into a tsetse fly area. They're attracted to bright, slow-moving objects, that pretty much described me, especially in my blue shirt. Eventually, I had to change my blue shirt. Those tsetse flies are as tough as old boots!

Angola is also a land of great riches. Its rivers and coastline are filled with perfectly polished stones – the ones ladies like wearing on their fingers: DIAMONDS!

Around Angola are teams of diggers and divers, working their butts off to find these shiny treasures.

→ **I sure hope Angola keeps on sparkling!**

ONE LOCAL ARMY MAN TAUGHT ME A CUNNING TRICK:
How to tell the difference between a tsetse fly and an ordinary fly – when you swat an ordinary fly, it keels over and falls off you. But when you swat a tsetse fly, it just does 10 push-ups – to show you it's BOSS – and then flies away.

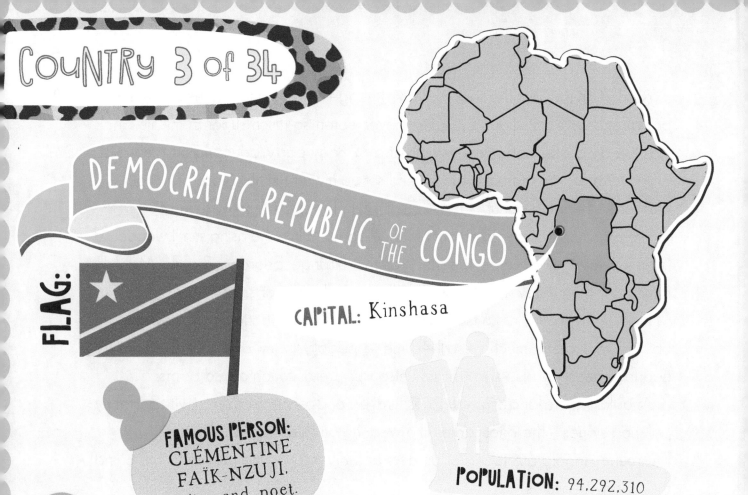

DEMOCRATIC REPUBLIC OF THE CONGO

FLAG:

CAPITAL: Kinshasa

FAMOUS PERSON:
CLÉMENTINE
FAÏK-NZUJI,
writer and poet.

POPULATION: 94,292,310

ADVENTURE ATTRACTIONS:
Virunga National Park to view
gorillas, chimpanzees and okapi;
Mount Nyiragongo, an active strato-
volcano containing the world's largest
lava lake.

LANGUAGES: French (official),
Kituba, Kikongo, Lingala,
Swahili, Tshiluba and others.

SPEAK:
'Good morning,
how are you?'
KITUBA:
'Mbote, wapi
faso?'

FABULOUS FOOD:
POULET À LA MOAMBE
Spicy chicken stew in a
palm butter sauce.

NATIONAL ANIMAL:
OKAPI

BORDER

INTO THE JUNGLE!

The long wooden motorboat chugged steadily across the wide river mouth to the Democratic Republic of the Congo. It was carrying my bike and me to the next leg of my journey.

Closer to shore, the sky grew dark and grey. WHOA! Gusts of winds blew spray into the boat, drenching all of us. The mighty Congo River and the even mightier Atlantic Ocean clashed as they collided into each other in the river mouth, like wrestlers locked in a fight.

The boat rolled over the heavy green swells and the foamy breakers. We were thrown into the air by a crashing wave.

WHOOSH! The boat was surfing down the swell. I was holding on for dear life!

I'd tied my foam bed mat to my bike, hoping it would float like a lifebuoy. If the boat sank, at least I'd be able to find it. Finally, the captain brought the creaking boat into shore. It felt as if the trip had taken forever!

Next, I cycled through soaking rains in the grassland and past large trees that soon became jungle. Night was falling – it was getting darker and darker. I was all alone and a bit scared. I struggled over thick, soft sand until I came to a long downhill stretch. I pushed off the top and sped faster and faster down the hill. It felt as if I was flying!

Then, in a flash, the front wheel was bogged down in sand. Now I really was flying... over the handlebars! SMASH!

I landed in a heap on the ground, covered in sweat and sand. I just lay there, exhausted and sore. But, I couldn't give up.

About an hour and a half later, I could see twinkling lights ahead of me. The border offices!

Pablo, a very friendly official, took me to a restaurant for dinner. He allowed me to sleep in his office that night and he even taught me some French: "MERCI, MON FRERE!" (Thank you, my brother!)

The next morning, as I saluted the national flag of the Democratic Republic of the Congo, my heart was filled with gratitude: I was making new friends in every country.

→ Soon I'd have an army of buddies all across Africa!

FLAG:

CAPITAL:
Brazzaville

REPUBLIC OF THE CONGO

POPULATION: 5,751,077

MOTTO:
Unity, Work, Progress

LANGUAGES:
French (official), Lingala,
Kituba, Kiteke, Akwa
and others.

CLIMATE:
Equatorial (north),
Tropical (center and south)

SPEAK:
'Good morning,
how are you?'
LINGALA
'Mbóte, ndenge nini?'

ADVENTURE ATTRACTIONS:
Odzala-Kokoua National
Park, to experience gorillas
and forest elephants;
Diosso Gorge, known as the
'Grand Canyon of the Congo',
to view the red rock ridges
and cliffs.

FABULOUS FOOD: FUMBWA
Wild spinach leaves (fumbwa)
cooked with palm oil, onions,
tomatoes, catfish and
peanut butter.

BORDER

BOOM BOOM! BADABOOM BOOM!

I slipped and skidded through the muddy jungle of the Congo Republic to the beating thuds of distant drums. Eventually, I spotted some kids making the most incredible music, laughing and dancing to the beat.

Later that hot, rainy night, I lay in my tent, listening to the monkeys chattering and the baboons barking fiercely in the leafy trees. I fell asleep, dreaming of floating in the cool, turquoise sea.

About an hour before sunrise, I felt something gently move under my back. At first, I thought that I was imagining it, or that I was going a bit crazy from my malaria tablets. But, something really had slithered sneakily beneath my groundsheet...

A SNAKE!
BOOM BOOM! BADABOOM BOOM!

This time it was my heart beating!

My pounding heartbeat sounded louder than the kids' drums. I'm sure they could hear it in the nearest village.

It was a matter of letting sleeping snakes lie, since all it wanted was a warm place to curl up in. So, I left the snake alone and it ignored me too, and the two of us enjoyed another 45 minutes' lie-in before the new day forced us out of the sack.

When the time came for me to crawl out, I did so very carefully, shoes on and with a watchful eye.

I collapsed my tent quickly and gently, then slowly pulled the groundsheet towards me. And there was my late-sleeping partner in full view. I'm colourblind, so I don't know exactly what its colours were, but there was a blocky yellow-and-black pattern on its body.

I didn't hang around to find out more! I really wanted to find the Atlantic Ocean, but... SQUELCH! THUD!

Every time I tried to cycle, I was sucked into the sticky mud and jungly bush until I crash-landed. So, I pushed my bike, and pushed and pushed. And then pushed some more. But I was able to cruise up and down some grassy hills, towards the crashing waves. Eventually, I stepped onto the beach under the beady-eyed gaze of thousands of crabs. I took off my shoes and socks, then ran to the water's edge, with the crab army encircling me. I felt like Gulliver arriving on the island of Lilliput!

SPLASH!

I threw myself into the sea, clothes and all. I didn't care:

After that sweaty, snakey jungle,

I WAS FREE IN THE SEA!

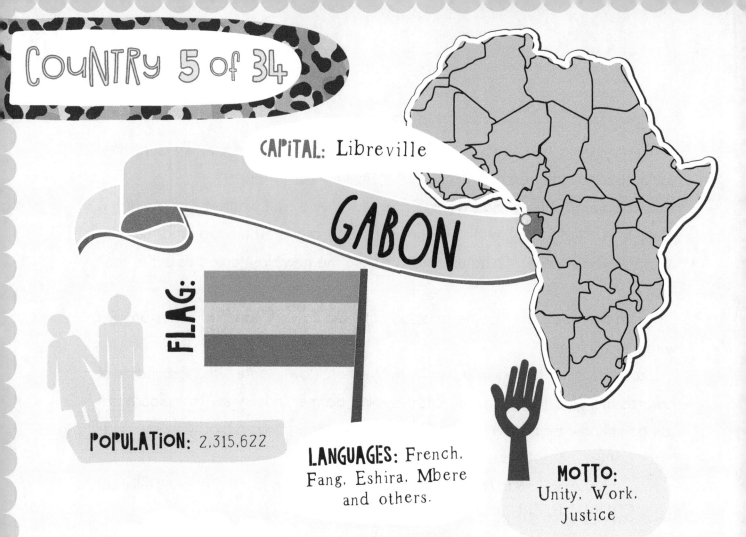

CAPITAL: Libreville

GABON

FLAG:

POPULATION: 2,315,622

LANGUAGES: French, Fang, Eshira, Mbere and others.

MOTTO: Unity, Work, Justice

NATIONAL ANIMAL: Black panther

SPEAK: 'Good morning, how are you?' FANG: 'Mbamba kiri, Wa ne mvé?'

ADVENTURE ATTRACTIONS: Cirque de Léconi. A deep red rock canyon surrounded by geological formations; Minkébé National Park. To view sandstone domes, giant hogs and forest elephants.

FABULOUS FOOD: POULET NYEMBWE Spicy chicken cooked in palm oil, onions, tomatoes, garlic and hot peppers, served with rice or fufu.

BORDER

 MAYUMBA

BISCUITS AND BESTIES

In the mountainous jungles of Gabon, I found some new BFFs. *Best Friends Forever*
And only some of them were people!

I was staying with my new friend Mahmoud. That night, after some scrumptious shortcake biscuits, I switched off my light and went to sleep.

BANG! CRASH!

I quickly shone my torch on the suspects. Ten giant rats, as big as small cats, were galloping over me and around my room in search of my left-over biscuits. HELP! Please don't take it personally, rats – but you guys FREAK ME OUT!

Next, I had to catch a boat up a snaking river. And on the deck, the people's supper waited: dried crocodile!

I cycled through forests of enormous trees, along rushing rivers and still lakes. In some places, the majestic trees were being chopped down.

I hope people remember that it is important to protect these magnificent green giants. C'MON, GUYS ⟶ they give us our oxygen!

By now, I was a brilliant biker – when travelling in straight lines. But my cornering still wasn't so hot – with that heavy, heavy bike. SPLAT!

I was approaching a cliff, and I just couldn't turn in time, and smashed into a wall of rock. My head was bleeding terribly. I was brave and patched up myself as best I could. But then I couldn't take it anymore – and I CRIED!

Boy, oh boy – I felt so good afterwards.

It was just what I had needed: a good old cry!

Soon, I was back in the saddle. The noisy thunder grumbled and rumbled overhead, and the first heavy drops of rain began to fall. I pitched my tent in a very special place – smack on top of the Equator. I was halfway up Africa!

The pouring rain pelted the tent as I enjoyed the sweetest pineapple that I've ever tasted.

THE EQUATOR

YOU KNOW, THE AMAZING THING ABOUT BEING AN ADVENTURER IS THAT THERE IS STILL SO MUCH TO DISCOVER, EVEN IN OUR MODERN WORLD!

LIBREVILLE

FLAG:

EQUATORIAL GUINEA

CAPITAL:
Malabo

POPULATION: 1,483,510

LANGUAGES:
Spanish (official),
French (official),
Portuguese (official),
Fang, Bube
and others.

MOTTO:
Unity, Peace, Justice

NATIONAL ANIMAL:
Giraffe

SPEAK:
'Good morning,
how are you?'
BUBE
'Ue a lövari,
ke soko?'

ADVENTURE ATTRACTIONS:
Bioko Biodiversity Protection
Program for primate and sea
turtle expeditions on Bioko
Island;
Monte Alén National Park
for hiking and viewing
elephants, chimpanzees
and gorillas.

FABULOUS FOOD:
SUCCOTASH
Lima beans, tomatoes
and corn cooked
in butter and
fresh herbs.

BORDER

MBINI

SOLDIERS AND SAILORS

The bright full moon beamed down on islands of mangrove forests as our boat chugged quietly away from the shore. We were boating off into the darkness... entering 'oil and gas country', where enormous wealth lies beneath the waves.

It took us just half an hour to get to Acalayong, a little village up the river.

That night, back on land, I snored gently in my tent on the chief's porch, exhausted by my travels.

The next day, I set off on a narrow road through the muddy jungles of Equatorial Guinea.

As night fell, I realised I could no longer see in front me.

PITCH DARKNESS... Just then, I was surprised to see a twinkling of lights just around the next bend. Was it a town? A city?

But the lights turned out to be paraffin lamps, hanging among a small cluster of huts.

An army captain and his men were living there. They were very kind, just like the people in so many of the other countries I had passed through.

The captain showed me a great spot to pitch camp, surrounded by fierce-looking soldiers, and a soldier in the hut next to me cooked a double supper – soft, puffy rice with bully beef and corn – so that there would be enough for me as well.

DELISH!

With a full belly heaving, courtesy of my new soldier friends, I cycled to the end of my journey through tiny Equatorial Guinea. I wish I could have taken some of these tough guys with me for later on in my African adventures.
I sure could have used their muscle in my battles ahead!

On to my next adventures in Cameroon!

CAMEROON

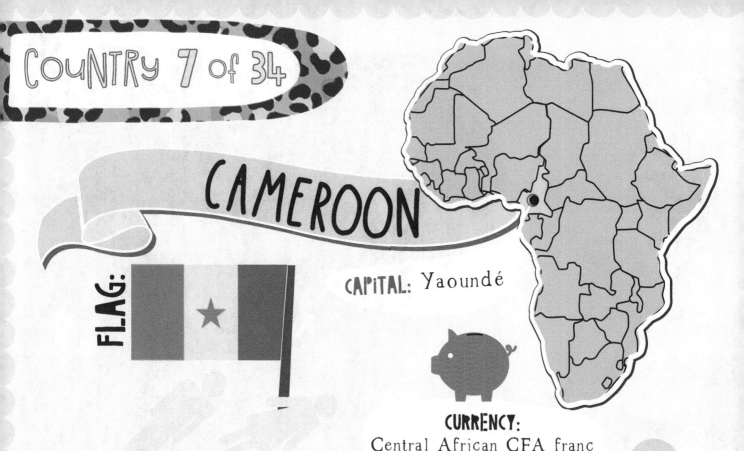

FLAG:

CAPITAL: Yaoundé

CURRENCY:
Central African CFA franc

POPULATION: 27,680,050

LANGUAGES:
French, English, German,
pidgin English, Fulfulde,
Ewondo and others.

ADVENTURE ATTRACTIONS:
Mount Cameroon hikes on an
active volcano; Chutes de la
Lobé waterfalls, that plunge
directly into the Atlantic Ocean.

MOTTO:
Peace, Work,
Fatherland

SPEAK:
'Good morning,
how are you?'
EWONDO:
'Mbembe amos,
one mvoé?'

FABULOUS FOOD: NDOLÉ
A bitter-leaf stew consisting of
beef or seafood, peanuts and
spinach, served with plantain,
fufu or rice.

BORDER

DOUALA

A WICKED VOLCANO AWAITED ME

In Cameroon, I was entering a country with an old German spell. YIKES! ⟶ I'd better watch out!

One bright day, I had a swim near the town's legendary Le Rocher de Loup, or Loop Rock. The locals believed that any person who swam out to the rock, and saw its centre, would never return to their home. I didn't look, to avoid being cast under that horrible spell – that's for sure!

I stopped at the first village and pitched my tent on the local mayor's front lawn.

His son, Alex, showed me around and took me down to the river for a swim. Then his mom cooked us a scrumptious meal: fufu corn and njama njama, a vegetarian dish of polenta and huckleberries. Talk about hospitality!

The next day, I cycled on, until I reached the Chutes de la Lobé, a freshwater waterfall that flows almost directly into the sea and drops straight into a tranquil lagoon.

PARADISE! I can't wait to go back one day.

I pedalled through huge palm plantations until I reached the seaside town of Limbe, that is built just south of an active volcano. The beach sand was black, from the years and years of lava deposits.

A strange but stunning sight.

As I continued down the road, I couldn't believe what I was seeing.

A slab of lava had flowed down the mountainside, blocking my path.

HECTIC!

➔ I had to dodge the lava with care.

WOW, where else in the world does someone ever have a close encounter like that?

NIGERIA

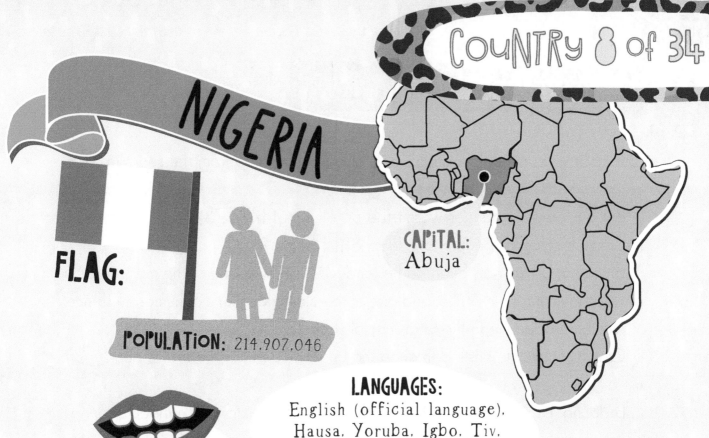

FLAG:

POPULATION: 214,907,046

CAPITAL:
Abuja

LANGUAGES:
English (official language),
Hausa, Yoruba, Igbo, Tiv,
Kanuri, Fulfulde and
others.

SPEAK:
'Good morning,
how are you?'
IGBO:
'Chi Abǫkwaa,
kedu kà ímèrè?'

FABULOUS FOOD:
JOLLOF RICE
A dish made with
long-grain rice, tomatoes,
onions, peppers and
spices.

ADVENTURE ATTRACTIONS:
Awhum Waterfalls; Ogbunike
Caves; Yankari National
Park and Wikki warm
water springs.

CURRENCY:
Nigerian Naira

NATIONAL ANIMAL: Black Crowned Crane

BORDER

BENIN CITY

A TRAVELLING ZOO ADVENTURE

Our boat sped through floating pools of oil, bubbling up from the sea. We were on our way to Nigeria, by water.

But our greatest danger wasn't the oil – it was PIRATES! They criss-crossed the seas, looking for people to kidnap. SHEESH!

Our boat driver was tough, so he landed us safely in one of the most densely populated countries in Africa, and one of the oldest locations of human existence.

My journey led me to the large city of Lagos in busy, bustling Nigeria.

Crowds of people hustled through the busy streets. I felt the sweat pouring off me as I pushed my bike.

Pedalling had become harder and harder – my bicycle's wheel bearings needed to be fixed. With my bike busted, I explored the city on foot.

Lagos, like the rest of Nigeria, had some gob-smacking sights. I was amazed at the size of the second-longest bridge in Africa. It's a massive 11.8km long and it is one of three bridges that connect the islands of Victoria, Ikoyi and Lagos to the mainland.

This reptilian bridge curved and stretched over the water like a giant snake.

Though the bridge was magnificent, I couldn't help thinking about something strange that I'd seen only a few days earlier. I'd stopped for a peaceful breakfast of coffee and buttered bread in the large town of Aga. As I was drinking my coffee, I spluttered in surprise. There, walking cheerily up to me, was a chimpanzee in a hat!

The chimp was walking upright, like a little person, dressed in a flowery shirt and shorts. He took off his hat, holding it out to me in the hope of getting a few coins.

The next minute, a man walked by, holding a huge male baboon on a very thin leash. It looked as if the baboon could snap it in a second!

LAGOS

Then, they were followed by something even stranger...

Two large, fully grown hyenas! Also held by almost invisible leashes. Their deep, menacing growls made ripples in my coffee as they passed. It was the first time I'd seen hyenas at really close range, and they were a scary sight - huge, hairy chests and massive jaws.

A TRAVELLING ZOO!

I wanted to cram my breakfast down my throat and get out of there at a rate of knots before something worse came by, but I had second thoughts and stayed put.

There was no chance of a quick getaway because the rest of the zoo was blocking my escape. The thought of two large, ill-tempered hyenas chasing after me like a pair of spotted guard dogs was simply too horrible to think about.

BENIN

CAPITAL:
Porto-Novo

FLAG:

POPULATION: 12,669,789

NATIONAL ANIMAL:
Leopard

LANGUAGES:
French, Fon, Fulfulde, Dendi, Mina, Yoruba and Bariba and others.

SPEAK:
'Good morning, how are you?'
FON:
'A fon a, a do gangi á?'

FAMOUS PERSON:
ANGÉLIQUE KIDJO
Singer-songwriter, actress and activist.

ADVENTURE ATTRACTIONS:
Ganvie Lake Village, to experience stilt houses and water markets; Pendjari National Park for wildlife and waterfall expeditions.

FABULOUS FOOD:
KULI-KULI
Fritters made from ground peanuts or groundnuts and spices, then deep fried in their own oils and served either hot or cold.

This was where many millions of people were captured along this entire region's coastline, and packed onto boats to be sold as slaves in faraway lands.

HONOURING OUR PAST

I rode my bike into Benin, knowing I would see a terribly sad memorial.

On a lonely beach is a massive arch, that has been built to remember them. It's called "THE DOOR OF NO RETURN" - as the slaves were marched off from here, to leave Africa forever. I was entering the 'Slave Coast' - stretching both east and west, for hundreds of kilometres.

Today, 200 years later, Benin is where you want to be if you're a cyclist. It's green and beautiful and cyclists have their own road lanes!

As I left the busy town of Cotonou, I saw a sign sticking out of a thick bush: "ZOO".

A zoo out here in the bush? Maybe a zoo was something else in Benin? Anyway, this I simply had to see!

It was a private zoo, with only a few animals, founded by the owner's grandfather. He still had two huge pythons, though, one of them over 3m long!

The zoo attendant lifted the huge python onto my shoulders. It was so heavy!

It wrapped its massive body around me, tightening itself grumpily around my neck.

SLITHERING AND TIGHTENING...

I started to sweat... then... SNAP!

The hungry python bared its ginormous fangs and lunged at my terrified face!

I grabbed it as it tried to slither out of my grip.

NO CHANCE! I wrestled its slippery body back with all my strength and screaming muscles.

I WAS WINNING!

Now, when I watch the video of my conversation with the python, I still break out in a cold sweat.

FLAG:

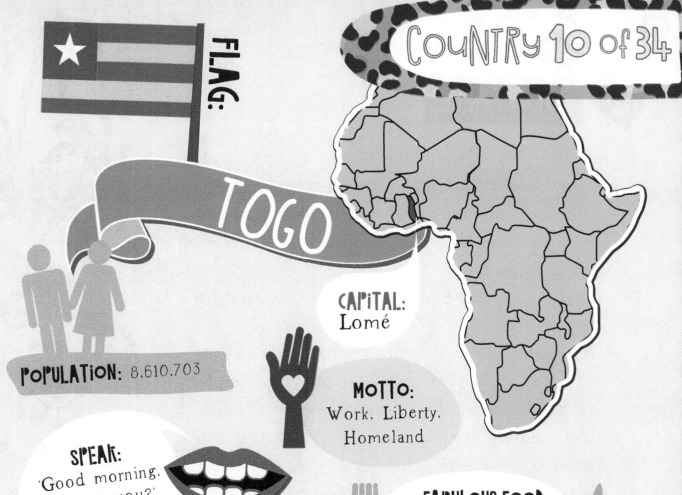

TOGO

CAPITAL:
Lomé

POPULATION: 8,610,703

MOTTO:
Work, Liberty,
Homeland

SPEAK:
'Good morning,
how are you?'
EWÉ:
'Mudobo,
afwa?'

FABULOUS FOOD:
AKUME
Maize flour porridge
usually served with pâtes
made from aubergine,
tomato, spinach
or fish.

ADVENTURE ATTRACTIONS:
Koutammakou UNESCO World
Heritage site, to view Batammariba
peoples' "takienta", earth tower
houses. Kpalime region, to climb
Mount Agou, the highest peak
in the country.

LANGUAGES:
French (Official), Ewé,
Kabiyé, Mina, Tem
and others.

NATIONAL ANIMAL: The African lion
AND the Pygmy Hippopotamus,
as there are no longer any African
lions living in the wild in Togo.

BORDER

SCARYVILLE!

Togo may be the skinniest little country in Africa – the whole country is only 160km wide – but it sure is a bit scary!

I strolled along Lomé's pretty promenade in the sunshine, watching people pedal past on cargo bicycles, delivering parcels all over the city.

A strong, warm wind gusted through the city, churning the dust into the air.

One of the delivery guys took time off to rest on a bench, and I photographed him, and when I looked at the photo later on, I was surprised to see that the background looked blurred, as if the day had been misty. But it was dust that blurred the background, not mist, and it was only then that I realised how strong the wind must have been.

The hot Harmattan winds swept into Lomé from the Sahara Desert towards the sea, bringing the dust clouds. When the dust reaches the coast, it becomes heavier as its particles absorb moisture from the cooler and more humid coastal atmosphere, and it settles to the ground.

It was hard to breathe in the hot, thick air. My eyes felt dry and crusty. Everything looked misty, hazy, mysterious...

As I left the city, an old man on a cargo bicycle appeared next to me, out of the cloudy haze. I cycled a little faster and so did the old man. I sped up again and the old man sped up again too.

RACE ON!

We battled on for 15km, pedalling furiously, panting away in the hot air. Then I spotted some fisherman in trouble. They were struggling to pull their gigantic nets into shore.

LOMÉ

I had to stop and lend a hand - if I carried on racing, they'd lose their catch.

WE PULLED AND PULLED AND PULLED!

By three o' clock in the afternoon, I arrived at the end of my journey in Togo.

Wow, this part of my journey had been fast and furious, but I'd got a lot done.

The scariest part of Togo, by far, were the voodoo markets. This, my friends, is where the local people believe that the animals have spirits! And their bones and body parts are preserved as magic medicine from the animal ancestors.

I FOUND IT SCARY!

But in all my travels, I was determined to respect every single belief with dignity.

FLAG:

GHANA

CAPITAL:
Accra

POPULATION: 32,176,538

SPEAK:
'Good morning,
how are you?'
DAGAARE:
'Fo angsoma,
fo be song?'

NATIONAL ANIMAL:
Tawny eagle

FABULOUS FOOD:
KELEWELE
Plantains seasoned with
peppers, ginger and
garlic, then fried.

ADVENTURE ATTRACTIONS:
Kakum National Park, to walk
the Canopy Walkway; Mole
National Park, for wildlife
viewing, including elephants,
leopards and lions.

LANGUAGES:
English (official), Akan,
Dagaare, Dangbe, Dagbane,
Ga, Kasem, Ewe and
Nzema and others.

BORDER

ACCRA

THE LAND OF THE BLACK STARS

Who are the Black Stars? The national Ghana soccer team, of course!

In Ghana's capital city, Accra, I saw something I'd never ever seen before.

André, my friend, said: "LOOK UP!" I looked up. I knew what these flying creatures were, but I couldn't believe it! Was it a bird? Was it a plane? Was it Superman?

No, they were BATS!

Hundreds of bats circling and swooping above the trees in the city's main park. Families were sitting below them, eating their picnics and whooping backwards and forwards on the swings, as though they didn't even notice them!

→This was very strange. Bats are supposed to spend the daylight hours in dark caves, resting for their night-time jaunts.

As I cycled on, I saw huge hills of white salt dotted alongside the road, with families and their donkey carts taking away small bits at a time.

THE SALT PLAINS! For as far as the eye could see, it was crystal white plains in every direction. And, can you believe it? I found a school among the salty hills. Their motto was 'Be Up and Doing'. What a great lesson!

Kids, you must always rely on yourself and your own abilities. That way, you'll "BE UP AND DOING" too.

FLAG:

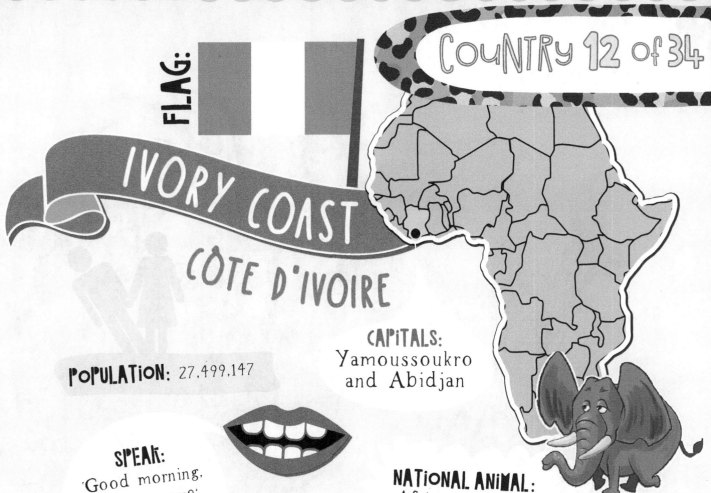

IVORY COAST
CÔTE D'IVOIRE

POPULATION: 27,499,147

CAPITALS:
Yamoussoukro
and Abidjan

SPEAK:
'Good morning,
how are you?'
KWA (BAOULÉ):
'Ahin, aho
oti kpa?'

NATIONAL ANIMAL:
African elephant

MOTTO:
Union, Discipline,
Work

LANGUAGES:
French, Kwa languages,
Kru languages, Senufo
languages, Mande
languages
and others.

FABULOUS FOOD:
ALLOCO
Ripe plantains fried
in palm oil, with a
spicy sauce made
of onions and
chillies.

ADVENTURE ATTRACTIONS:
Tai National Park, to view
pygmy hippopotami, leopards
and chimps; waterfalls at Les
Cascades de Man.

BORDER

ABIDJAN

Part of life's adventure is to munch, devour, gobble, wolf down... TO EAT!
But I had no idea what I was about to be faced with on my dinner plate.

My journey into the Ivory Coast began as I headed into the hilly border region, sweating like a fountain in the terrible heat.

On the path, I came across a teenager, carrying on his shoulder what I reckoned must be the biggest pineapple on earth.

It was a monstrous pineapple, as big as a watermelon!

As I cycled on, I stopped to ask for directions to get some fresh water. A truck driver gave me a sachet of great-tasting red ice called 'bissap', a mixture of boiled hibiscus flower and sugar. It gave me all the "VOOMA" I needed!

My food adventures continued in Abidjan, as I discovered that Abidjanians like to eat their bats instead of just looking at them.

Treichville also introduced me to new types of West African food – rat and bat stews!

I don't think I would have eaten either of them at home, but they tasted the same as most other types of meat.

Then, it came to my last meal in the Ivory Coast.

I stopped at a dusty little restaurant and ordered my usual meal, 'riz et sauce'.

My mouth watered as the waitress brought me a bowl of fluffy rice with the meat on top. The rice, soaked in pepper sauce and the meat's juices, smelled irresistible.

I ate it with gusto – it tasted great! When I thanked the waitress, she told me it was the freshest meat in the kitchen... MONKEY MEAT!

I felt a bit bad, munching one of those cheeky little critters I often wave at in the trees.

HAVE YOU EATEN SOMETHING UNUSUAL?

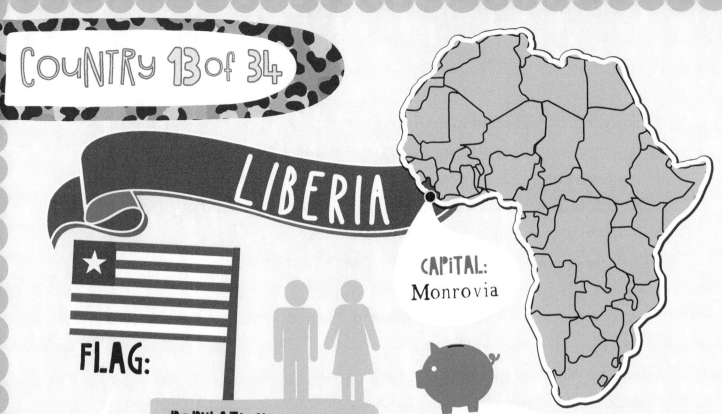

LIBERIA

FLAG:

CAPITAL:
Monrovia

POPULATION: 5.261.101

CURRENCY:
Liberian Dollar

LANGUAGES:
English (official language), Mande, Kwa, Mel and Gola language groups and others.

SPEAK:
'Good morning, how are you?'
GOLA:
'Markeer, de mun tuvo?'

FAMOUS PERSON:
ELLEN JOHNSON SIRLEAF
Known as Africa's 'Iron Lady', Liberia's first elected female president. She was awarded a Nobel Peace Prize in 2011.

ADVENTURE ATTRACTIONS:
Sappo National Park, home to the African golden cat, pygmy hippopotamus, forest elephant, leopard and three species of pangolin; Robertsport, the best surfing spot in Liberia.

FABULOUS FOOD:
TORBORGEE
Spicy stew of dried meat or fish, torborgee beans and palm oil.

BORDER

MONROVIA

OH BOY, A SERIOUSLY DANGEROUS PLACE!

My plan to circumnavigate Africa by bicycle definitely sounded crazy to some people, especially when they found out my journey would take me through Liberia.

When I arrived in Liberia, it was a country that had just been through a long civil war – countrymen fighting each other in a terrible mess. I knew it could be a dangerous part of my adventure, and it was.

The countryside was green, hilly jungle with bright red soil.

Before I knew it, the WORST happened: I was captured. I was surrounded by a whole gang of mad-looking young soldiers.

In a flash, they had grabbed me and my bike, and dragged me into a home-made prison cell. They couldn't understand why I was there, especially since the country was still at war.

For hours and hours, they refused to set me free. I was trapped, like a prisoner!

Eventually, they let me go. And boy, did I then ride away fast... all the way to the capital city, Monrovia, feeling shocked and frightened.

I stayed with a wonderful man, Guy Guerneas, who worked with the refugees in Liberia.

He told me that I had to catch a ride on a truck to the border of Sierra Leone. I was disappointed because I had wanted to cover every centimetre of the route on my bicycle, but I had to be safe to continue my journey into the rest of Africa. YOU CAN'T ALWAYS GET WHAT YOU WANT.

But I was safe and grateful, and about to start moving in the right direction again.

The United Nations helped me navigate this dangerous country. They calmed me down, gave me places to sleep and called ahead - finding me places to stay and be safe on my journey.

WHEW!

FLAG:

SIERRA LEONE

POPULATION: 8,252,672

CAPITAL:
Freetown

SPEAK:
'Good morning,
how are you?'
KRIO:
'Monin o,
aw yu du?'

FABULOUS FOOD:
GROUNDNUT
STEW
Chicken and
vegetables with ground
nuts, often cashews
or peanuts.

NATIONAL ANIMAL:
Chimpanzee

LANGUAGES:
English (official),
Krio, Mende,
Temne, Limba
and others.

ADVENTURE ATTRACTIONS:
Tiwai Island Wildlife
Sanctuary for pygmy
hippopotamus sightings,
Mount Bintumani (Loma
Mansa), highest peak in
Sierra Leone, for hiking
and mountaineering.

FAMOUS PERSON:
ABIOSEH NICOL (DAVIDSON SYLVESTER
HECTOR WILLOUGHBY NICOL),
Academic, diplomat, physician, writer and
poet. First African to graduate with First
Class Honours from the University of
Cambridge and the first African elected as
a fellow of Cambridge University. He later
became the Under-Secretary-General
of the United Nations.

BORDER

AN OLD FRIEND, OUT OF THE BLUE!

Freetown is wonderful, as pretty as Cape Town!

Green forests, gentle hills and blue, blue seas... if Freetown had been in South Africa, it would have competed with Cape Town as the No. 1 tourist destination in Africa!

It has a gorgeous coastline, a natural harbour, many golden beaches, a river lagoon, seafood restaurants, luxury hotels and a chimpanzee sanctuary, to honour the national animal!

But the best part was when I unexpectedly met an old friend again.

I had arranged on the phone to visit a company. When my old friend Julius walked through the door, my jaw dropped nearly to the floor!

You see, Julius wasn't just my friend, he was also my hero.

When I was an 18-year-old boy in 44 Parachute Brigade in the army, one of my officers was Major Julius Lloyd of the Special Forces.

He was a living legend and everyone's model of a good soldier, the sort of man that you would want next to you when the bullets were flying. And here, 12 years later, we were meeting again, in Freetown of all places!

He insisted that I stay with him for as long as I was in Freetown, and I accepted. It would be the safest place to lay my head in all of Sierra Leone!

One of the saddest places I had seen in all of Africa was a special hospital for victims of war. These were super-brave young boys and girls, men and women, who had to get through life, severely injured.

And with smiles on their faces. WOW. How courageous they were!

FREETOWN

GUINEA

FLAG:

CAPITAL:
Conakry

POPULATION: 13,747,232

SPEAK:
'Good morning,
how are you?'
SUSU:
'I kena, tana mu
na?'

LANGUAGES:
French (official),
Fula, Malinké, Susu,
Kissi, Kpelle and
Toma and others.

CURRENCY:
Guinean Franc

NATIONAL ANIMAL:
African Forest Elephant

FABULOUS FOOD:
POULET YASSA
Chicken pieces
marinated in onion
and lemon, served
with rice.

ADVENTURE ATTRACTIONS:
Mount Nimba Strict Nature
Reserve, for viewing
chimpanzees in the wild.
Chutes de Kambadaga,
hiking and waterfalls.

BORDER

CONAKRY

INTO A CRAZY WORLD OF MISUNDERSTANDING

My journey in Guinea showed me how important it is to be able to talk to each other. To understand people – even if we speak different languages.

How many languages can you speak, by the way?

I can tell you, Western Africa has so many different languages that sometimes it's difficult to understand one another. It's like a crazy, constantly changing jigsaw puzzle of people, languages, religions and lifestyles.

Sometimes it was almost impossible to communicate properly at all.

In Conakry, my friend Iqbal took me to a shop to phone my girlfriend, Vasti. This was my chance to have a good heart-to-heart talk with her.

But, the young men in charge of the shop took too much of my money for the call, that should have been much cheaper.

Iqbal was angry. He thought that the young men were cheating me out of my money.

He told them to give me some of the money back, but they wouldn't listen.

One of the men tried to punch Iqbal, but he didn't know that Iqbal was an expert boxer! Iqbal gave him a crisp right hook to the ear...

A ding-dong fist fight!

Some police vans came flying up the road, lights flashing and sirens screaming. We were loaded into the van and taken to the police station.

At the station, some local leaders listened to our stories. After talking among themselves for 10 minutes, they said that they were very sorry and embarrassed by the young man's behaviour.

He was fined more money than the amount he'd taken.

And we should always rather use our words than our fists!

You see, we should always be honest and fair.

GUINEA-BISSAU

FLAG:

CAPITAL: Bissau

POPULATION: 2,047,619

LANGUAGES:
Portuguese (official),
Guinea-Bissau Creole,
Balanta, Fula, Mandjak
and others.

SPEAK:
General greeting
BALANTA:
'Abala, lite
utchole.'

CLIMATE: Tropical

MOTTO:
Unity, Struggle,
Progress

ADVENTURE ATTRACTIONS:
João Vieira e Poilão
Marine National Park,
a nesting location for
three species of turtle;
Saltinho waterfalls, for
views of the rapids and
fishing downstream in
calmer waters.

FABULOUS FOOD:
ABACATE COM TUNA
Ripe avocados, tuna, grated
coconut, evaporated milk and
tomato sauce, mixed together
and served in the avocado
skins with lemon
wedges.

BORDER

BUBAQUE

A REAL BUMMER!

I was on my way to Guinea-Bissau by pirogue – a small boat.

The journey would take two days and the boat had 25 other people on board. It was a very tight squeeze!

I had to take all my own food and extra water.

That night I tried to sleep, but I was too squashed in, especially since my bike was crammed next to me – with my pedals jabbing into my ribs.

I tried to balance on my side on the edge of the boat, to get some sleep, but it was very narrow. An unexpected roll would toss me into the sea!

Then, I had a bigger problem – a very urgent problem...

There were no toilets on board, and I really needed to go!

I had no choice – I had to do what everyone else was doing.

I waited until most people were asleep. I shimmied to the darkest, quietest space, pulled my trousers down and hung my butt over the edge!

EEEUUUWW!

We spent all the next day at sea, too.

I was so bored. The sun baked down on us, the outboard motor droned on and on, and the swells splashed endlessly on the sides of the pirogue.

We were on the boat for 38 hours!

But eventually, we arrived in Bubaque, in the heart of the archipelago – that is like a whole family of little islands.

We had to stay on the island for two days, waiting to catch the next pirogue to Guinea-Bissau. It was fun fishing off the pier with the island kids, and they were expert fishermen!

I finally arrived in Guinea-Bissau. It's a tiny country. If you travel north, it just gets drier and drier, like a desert.

As I cycled closer and closer to the border, I was getting a lot of funny looks. People thought there was something very peculiar about a South African calmly pedalling around on a bicycle in their wild, dry country, all on his own. Then I was at the border, and ready for a slightly less smelly few weeks ahead.

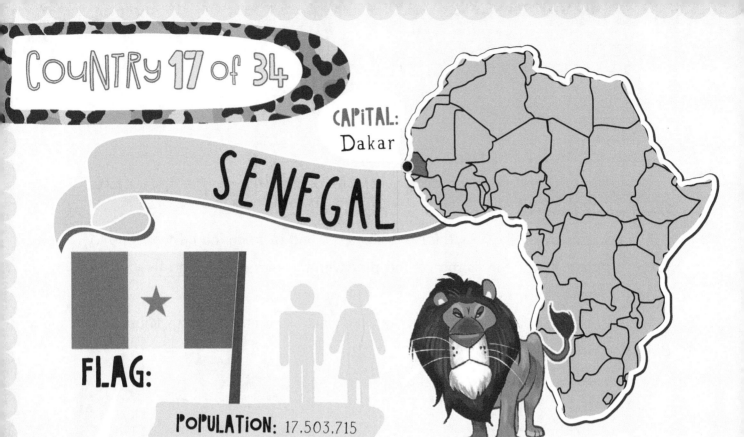

CAPITAL:
Dakar

SENEGAL

FLAG:

POPULATION: 17,503,715

NATIONAL ANIMAL:
Lion

LANGUAGES:
French (official),
Wolof, Pulaar,
Mandinka, Balan-
ta-Ganja, Mandjak
and others.

MOTTO:
One People,
One Purpose,
One Faith

SPEAK:
'Good morning?'
WOLOF:
'Jama nga
fanaan?'

ADVENTURE ATTRACTIONS:
Parc National du Delta du
Saloum (national park), for
water tours of the mangroves,
salt marshes, islands and
woodlands;
Île de N'Gor, a tiny island,
for surfing and beaches.

FABULOUS FOOD:
THIÉBOUDIENNE
Fresh or dried fish
and spices, with
purée made of
tomato, onion, garlic
and chilli,
and rice.

BORDER

DAKAR

A LAND OF SURPRISES

Can anyone guess what the favourite crop in Senegal is?

PEANUTS! Black Cat Peanut Butter Country, YEAH!

And, they're MAD about sport.

Senegal is a country of flamboyant colour and music. I had a wonderful time in Dakar. And I got there on a fabulous new road, smooth and fast.

I celebrated with a cup of warm camel's milk! What did it taste like?

SWEET, AND SALTY, AND CREAMY! Like a new milkshake on the Wimpy menu!

My friend Nic and I roared around on his big scrambler motorcycle, seeing great sights and even riding the waves at Ngor beach.

I got dumped and tossed around like a piece of driftwood in them waves that day, but soon got my eye in and had a great surf.

Just when I thought my visit couldn't be any better, I received some fantastic news: Vasti, my girlfriend, was coming to visit!

I waited impatiently for her flight to arrive.

Finally, the plane touched down.

I was so excited. My love was at my side again!

YABBADABBADOO!

NGOR

We spent three days eating huge hotel breakfasts, watching rugby and buying snacks in the city. I even showed off my new French vocabulary!

Like "JE T'AIME, VASTI!"

When it was time for her to fly home, I was very sad. I watched her plane get smaller and smaller, then finally vanish into the blue distance.

It was a tough moment for me, but even though Vasti was gone, I'd had three glorious days with her...

THE GAMBIA

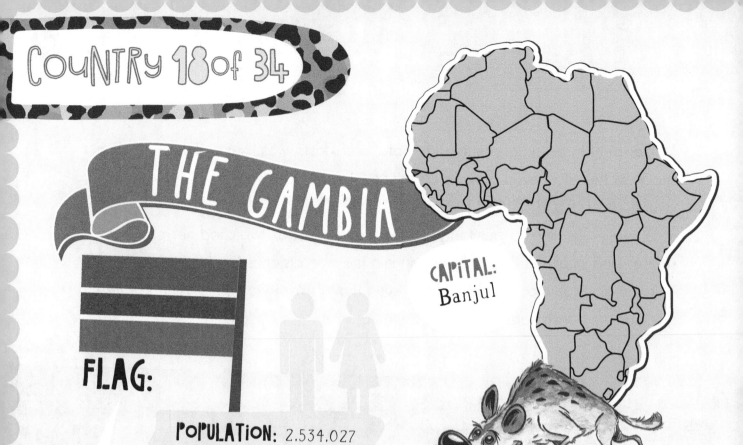

FLAG:

CAPITAL:
Banjul

POPULATION: 2,534,027

LANGUAGES:
English (official),
Mandinka, Fula
(Pulaar), Wolof
and others.

NATIONAL ANIMAL:
Spotted hyena

SPEAK:
A Morning
greeting in
PULAAR:
'A Waalii
e jam?'

CLIMATE:
Sub-tropical

ADVENTURE ATTRACTIONS:
Kunta Kinteh Island, to
explore the ruins of the
old British slave fort;
Kachikally Crocodile
Pool, a local sacred site,
to view crocodiles.

FABULOUS FOOD:
DOMODA
Peanut stew made
with tomato paste,
mustard, onions and
sweet potato or
pumpkin.

BORDER

BANJUL

THE TINIEST COUNTRY OF ALL

The Gambia is a tiny country, that is wedged like a dagger into the middle of the Sengalese Coast. BUT GUESS WHAT? The Gambians spoke English – so there was less sign language and so many jokes we could all understand, for once!

In The Gambia, I would soon track down the most famous clothing market in all of West Africa. This is where they are masters of the batik craft.

First, you melt some wax, like from a candle. Then you paint it onto a shirt in particular patterns that you like. Then you dye the shirt in your favourite colours. And guess what? The wax stops the parts you painted from being dyed. TA DA!

In this amazing market were also the WWF of Africa: WRESTLING!

At the national stadium, wrestlers grapple and grunt in fighting contests. I was

almost tempted to take part too, but I still had a l-o-n-g way to ride, so getting injured would be a bad idea.

Before acting like a tourist, though, I had to find a special person to fix something that I really needed...

MY CYCLING SHOES!

My leather cycling shoes were falling apart, which made pedalling very uncomfortable.

I found a cobbler on the side of the road.

I was worried that the shoes were too badly broken to be fixed. The cobbler just laughed and invited me to sit on the pavement next to him.

It took some serious surgery, but the cobbler sewed the shoes into very good shape. BY HAND!

There are some very crafty people in the world!

Do you have any precious handmade crafts from Africa in your home?

MAURITANIA

FLAG:

POPULATION: 4,860,078

CAPITAL: Nouakchott

LANGUAGES:
Modern Standard Arabic (official), Hassaniyya Arabic, French, Pulaar, Soninke, Wolof, Bambara and others.

SPEAK:
'Good morning, how are you?'
HASSANIYYA ARABIC:
'Ish haal issbaah, sh'halak?'

ADVENTURE ATTRACTIONS:
Richat Structure, known as the 'Eye of Africa', a geological phenomenon created by the erosion of a geological dome; camping at the Ben Amera, one of the largest monoliths in the world.

MOTTO:
Honour, Fraternity, Justice

CURRENCY:
Mauritanian Ouguiya

FABULOUS FOOD:
HAKKO
Ground bean leaf sauce, served over couscous.

 BORDER

NOUAKCHOTT   ATAR

INTO THE DUST BOWL

As I rode north, it got drier. And dustier. And desertier. **Is that even a word?**

I was now surrounded by the seemingly endless desert in Mauritania. Like a ship afloat at sea, with no land in sight. The land was flat, but the wind blew in only one direction – towards me. I ached in the heat, but there was an awesome beauty to the endless great mountains of golden sand.

In case you think there can be nothing crazier than someone cycling through umpteen kilometres of empty desert, there are lots of us mad people in the world.

I could see someone coming towards me on the long, dusty road.

He was moving fast, almost gliding towards me. He was wearing a biker jacket, a balaclava, and an umbrella over his shoulder, like Mary Poppins...

HE WAS ON ROLLERBLADES! He was rollerblading from Atar to Nouakchott for the sheer fun of it, with the wind at his back.

He was very friendly, and we shared a cup of sweet Mauritanian tea as I told him about my adventures. Maybe he was so inspired that he decided to keep on rollerblading till he reached Cape Town.

WESTERN SAHARA

FLAG:

POPULATION: 622,530

CAPITAL:
Laayoune/
El-Aaiún

LANGUAGES:
Hassaniyya Arabic,
Moroccan Arabic,
Modern Standard Arabic,
Spanish, French and
Berber and
others.

CLIMATE:
Desert

SPEAK:
'Greetings, how
are you?'
MOROCCAN
ARABIC:
'Salam 'leykum,
kif halek?'

ADVENTURE ATTRACTIONS:
Kitesurfing, windsurfing and
surfcasting at Dakhla.

CURRENCY:
Moroccan
Dirham

FABULOUS FOOD:
MEIFRISA
Rabbit, lamb or
camel stew, with
onion and garlic,
served with
unleavened
bread.

BORDER

AD DAKHLA

SAND, SAND AND MORE SAND

I arrived at Laayoune just in time to battle my way through three huge sandstorms that brought all traffic to a halt.

For the first time, I really appreciated my turban – a lifesaver that kept at least half a kilogram of sand out of my ears.

The wind howled and screamed around the city, blasting everything with sand.

In the desert, the days are HOT, HOT, HOT. But at night, it's COLD, COLD, COLD! Just like the Karoo in my own home country, South Africa. It's so dry your lips crack.

And so does your sense of humour...

BOUJDOUR

One evening, I put up my tent and made sure that it would stay up in the icy, gale-force wind. As I huddled inside, my heart sank. I had left my sleeping bag outside, strapped to my bike.

I was very tired – I didn't feel like facing that icy blast of wind again. I wrapped myself in my small plastic tarpaulin, hoping it would keep me warm.

I tossed and turned on the rocky floor of the tent, shivering.

Eventually, I gave up. I climbed out of my tent, grabbed my sleeping bag and snuggled in.

I SLEPT LIKE A KING!

But my darkest moment in almost eight months came when I got some terrible news from home: my favourite dog, a boxer named Murphy, had died. I would never be able to say goodbye to him properly. But I knew his spirit was free. I sent him my love on the wings of the Harmattan desert wind.

LAAYOUNE

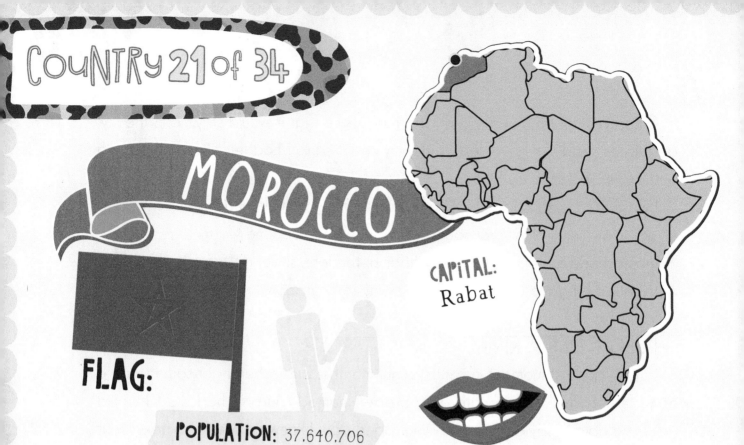

MOROCCO

FLAG:

CAPITAL:
Rabat

POPULATION: 37,640,706

LANGUAGES:
Modern Standard Arabic (official), Berber/ Tamazight, Moroccan Arabic, French, Spanish, English and others.

CLIMATE:
Mediterranean

SPEAK:
'Good morning, how are you?'
CENTRAL ATLAS TAMAZIGHT/ BERBER:
'Sbah lxir, manik an tgut?'

NATIONAL ANIMAL:
Barbary lion

ADVENTURE ATTRACTIONS:
Ziplining or walking the suspension and tightrope bridges across the Atlas Mountain gorge; sand-boarding down the Erg Chebbi dunes, Marzouga.

FABULOUS FOOD:
TAGINE -BEEF OR CHICKEN
Cooked in a tagine, served with couscous.

BORDER

AGADIR

CASSABLANCA

EXOTIC AND SPICY

There was sand in my eyes. Sand right up my nostrils. Sand in my ears. Sand in my bum! AAAARRGGH!

Oh boy! I was entering the world's largest desert. And there are no roads!

Dunes surrounded me on all sides. That was it.

NO PEOPLE. NO ROAD. NO SIGNPOSTS, NO NOTHING. Only some tyre tracks in the sand.

So, I slogged along, pushing my bike in the tracks. PLOD, PLOD, PLOD...

Eventually, I saw a building – a desert workshop, offering to repair passing cars before they continued into "THE BIG THIRST".

But I didn't need a car workshop. I needed a bicycle mechanic!

The fine desert sand had crept into every moving part of my bicycle, causing it to crunch apart with every pedal.

My gears, my chain – all were invaded by sand, like ants going mad on a sticky sweet.

Riding my bike was like trying to chew through a sandwich that had fallen onto the beach.

But my prayers for help were answered!

I came across a group of French teenagers. They were naughty young men, who had been sent on a youth camp by the French government, to make them forget their naughty ways in the desert.

In the end, they gave me a ride up to the city of Rabat. (It sounds like 'rabbit'.) And there, the South African embassy gathered a team of all the best bike experts in the capital to give my bike a doctor's visit – a full hospital check-up, head to toe.

It felt as if I had a new bike!

RABAT   FÉS   OUJDA

I also needed a complete makeover – I was wild, woolly, and dirty after battling the desert.

Before I set out again, I met a famous rally driver, who had once won the most famous rally in the world: the Paris-Dakar Rally. One day, maybe I'll become a rally driver – instead of having to chug and puff my every step with my own engine.

In Rabat, I met the famous desert horsemen and horsewomen of Morocco:
THE DESERT WARRIORS OF THE FANTASIA FESTIVAL.
Their job was to act out a famous war dance, firing old musket guns into the air – while their horses galloped as fast as they could run.

The soldiers and horses charged across a field together, just like in the old wars before cars and tanks.

→ A centuries-old tradition.

Next, I was taken to the 800-year-old, 12th century Tower of Hassan. The workers began building in the year 1195!

After this, I rode my bike into the famous city of Casablanca. In its heart, right in the middle, was the Medina (Old City) – more than 1,000 years old, with its huge surrounding wall, breath-taking in its size and beauty. Inside was a labyrinth of alleys. And the second largest working mosque in Africa, the King Hassan II Mosque. It was built by over 10 000 workers, and has a 210m-high minaret, the highest in the whole of Africa.

I sat on woven pillows, gobbling down a lunch of dates, vegetables, bread and tender meat.

Waiting for me were the craggy Atlas Mountains, with their majestic cliffs, between the desert and the sea.

My poor old bike. I had eight punctures in 20km. Eventually, I couldn't fix a single puncture more, and fell asleep in an old ruin on a hill, on a bed of stones and scorpions.

Phew, the next day I was so glad to see bee farms everywhere. And hundreds of stalls selling honey along the road. ENERGY. YEEHA!

But huge sandstorms were so thick with sand that even cars had to stop dead in the streets. My turban kept about a bucketful of sand out of each of my ears.

The sky was dark with flying sand, a policeman didn't even see me walk right in front of him.

I was determined to make it. "INSHALLAH". God willing

One night, a campsite was too expensive, so I made my bed for the night in a digger loader's bucket.

I was becoming the toughest desert rider in Africa!

FLAG:

HALF WAY

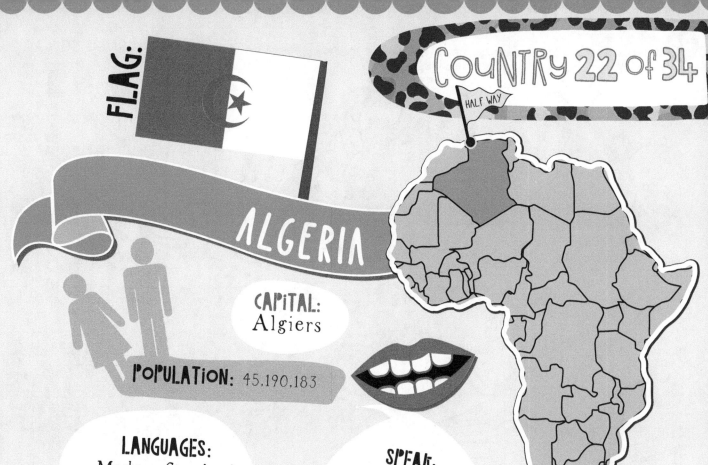

ALGERIA

CAPITAL:
Algiers

POPULATION: 45,190,183

LANGUAGES:
Modern Standard Arabic (official), Tamazight/Berber (official), Algerian Arabic, Hassaniyya Arabic, French and others.

SPEAK:
'Greetings, how are you?'
ALGERIAN ARABIC:
'Axir, was̆ rak?'

CURRENCY:
Algerian Dinar

NATIONAL ANIMAL:
Fennec fox

ADVENTURE ATTRACTIONS:
Tassili n'Ajjer National Park, to experience a sandstone mountain range, rock arches, rock art and prehistoric cave paintings; Les Grottes de Beni Add, Tlemcen, to explore the 57m deep caves and mineral formations.

FABULOUS FOOD:
MAKROUDH
A traditional pastry dessert, consisting of deep-fried semolina stuffed with dates or almonds and dipped in honey.

BORDER

ORAN   ALGIERS   CONSTANTINE

CAKES AND KINDNESS

Can you believe it? Algeria is the country in Africa where they all eat WHAT for breakfast? CAKE!

I already LOVED this country.

My first sight of Algeria were the honey-coloured cliffs of Ghazaouet, where houses are chiselled into the rocky coastline of North Africa.

And when my mouth dried up with the heat of the desert, there were always melons and pawpaws. I ate so many to rehydrate my body I felt my stomach would pop.

Soon, I crossed the Greenwich Meridian – check this on the map too. This was the half- way point of my journey, roughly 18,000km. Every turn of my wheel was now taking me back down the length of Africa to Cape Town.

I had lost 14kg, and averaged 111km per cycling day. This is the same as doing a Cape Town Cycle Tour every day for nine months. Except, my journey was worse – the extreme heat of 46°C, biting cold and dangerous lands. And often without money, food or water.

But in Algeria, they know how to have a party in style. The weddings there last three days. And if you are very rich, you begin on a Monday, and carry on until the actual ceremony on Saturday – a six-day wedding!

I began the crazy journey, up, up, up hundreds of hills, to the city of Constantine – one of the oldest continuously inhabited cities in Africa.

This ancient place was first built in 203BC by the Phoenicians, who built a city of great splendour – like a castle in a fairy tale.

In AD311, it was destroyed in a war between two Roman emperors, Maxentius and Domitius Alexander.

Eventually, it was named after Constantine the Great.

And here I found another magnificent munch: ALGERIAN PIZZAS, WITH FENNEL SAUSAGE.

One man was so kind that he paid for my pizza with his last money and had nothing for himself. This is the tradition there: travellers always come first.

One day, if he comes to my home in Cape Town, I will feed him all the food in my fridge.

Total of 18,000km
Average of 111km per day!
Lost 14kg

More than 400 days from home
More than 18 000 km to go

HALF WAY

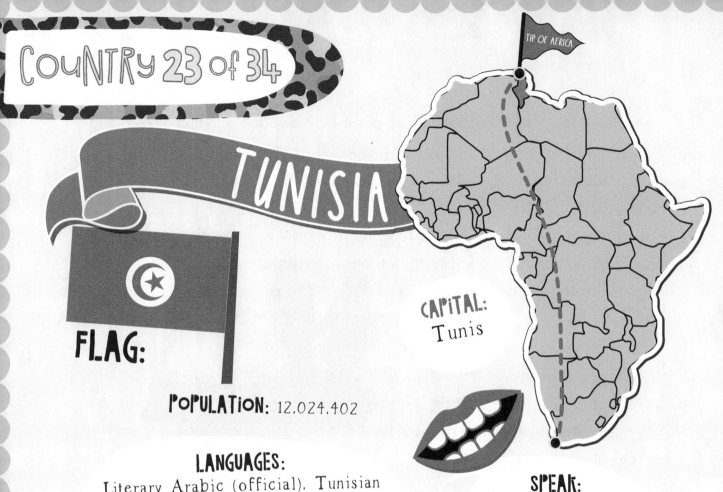

TUNISIA

FLAG:

CAPITAL:
Tunis

POPULATION: 12.024.402

LANGUAGES:
Literary Arabic (official). Tunisian Darija/Arabic (national). Berber. French. English. Italian and others.

SPEAK:
'Good morning. how are you?'
TUNISIAN ARABIC:
'Sbā khĭr, nija hālik?'

CLIMATE:
Mediterranean in the north, semi-arid to desert in the south.

MOTTO:
Freedom, Dignity, Order and Justice

ADVENTURE ATTRACTIONS:
Hot-air ballooning in the Tunisian Balloons Festival in Sfax and Tunis: diving in the seas off Hammamet to view shipwrecks. deep-sea caves and coral reefs.

FABULOUS FOOD:
BRIK
A pastry shell (malsouka) that is filled with egg, parsley and tuna. then folded into a triangle and garnished with lemon juice.

BORDER

TUNIS

FROM TOE TO TIP

I freewheeled down a mountain, into my first town in Tunisia.
If all roads were downhill, I could ride all day long!

Which do you prefer: riding uphill, or downhill?

The people of Tunisia LOVE tourists – who bring their money from all over the world. The first 'tourists' were the Phoenicians – about 3,000 years ago! They came in their beautiful wooden ships and they were the best mariners in the ancient world.

Next time, maybe I should circle Africa by boat. But first, I had to make it by bicycle.

As I pedalled over the last tall hill on my way to Tunis, I caught sight of the lakes surrounding the capital.

In every old North African city, you'll find the medina - a cobbled jungle of alleyways and markets that hasn't changed in hundreds of years. But there are also some very modern streets. At the top of one is a mini version of the famous Arc de Triomphe in Paris, called Bab El Bhar or the French Gate - the French built it when they ruled Tunisia. There's also a tiny community of Jewish people, though the country is 98% Muslim.

IT WAS A SPECIAL MOMENT. I'd reached the top of Africa! I'd cycled from Africa's southernmost city to its northern most one.

TIP OF AFRICA

It's a funny thing - at that moment, Cape Town and Tunis didn't seem all that far apart. But on a map, you can see that these two cities are tip to toe from each other. If you look on our map, you'll see Cape Town is Africa's 'toe', and Tunis is the highest hair on the top of its head!

The actual VERY top is a place called Bizerte. Here I caught a piece of driftwood, floating on the Mediterranean Sea, and decided to take it home with me, to keep FOREVER. To prove I was actually there...

Sidi Bou Said is an amazing place, with colourful doorways and real Tunisian coffee shops where you sit on pillows like some old-time sultan.

I found the real Tunisian coffee a bit tricky to drink, though. It was as thick as mud, and I felt as if I was chewing it. I didn't know that you're not supposed to chugalug the lot in one gulp, in South African style. You're only supposed to drink the runny bit at the top.

TIP OF AFRICA

BIZERTE   SIDI BOU SAID

Anyway, I said goodbye to the owner, my teeth full of brown coffee sludge. He managed to keep a straight face, but I'm sure he was laughing at me...

And that's not the only time someone in Tunisia thought I was a bit strange.

Along the stretch of road to Bir Sheba, I found my first (and only) pet of my journey.

I was battling my way through icy rain, and I was soaked to the skin.

Groups of little field mice were shivering by the side of the road. Some had moved onto the tarmac to absorb some of the earlier sun's warmth. One little mouse was sitting on the yellow line, shivering, and I knew that he was a dead duck as soon as the next car came along. I scooped him up, dried him off with my oily chain-rag and stuck him into my dry jacket pocket.

His name was Russell.

Russell immediately became part of my journey.

He shared my food and even sat with me in fancy roadside garage restaurants.

I was soon so fond of him that I could see myself riding into the Waterfront in Cape Town, holding him aloft for the cheering crowd to see.

But Russell had other ideas.

He was standing up on his hind legs, nibbling on a piece of carrot during my lunch in a shop, when he suddenly decided that it was time to go. He took off like a rocket, landed on the floor, rolled onto his stomach, and scurried away.

I ran after him to save him from himself, dodging between the petrol pumps with the cleats on my cycling shoes clacking loudly.

I must have looked like a total madman as I darted around, hunched over like Quasimodo, snatching at thin air and shouting instructions to Russell.

Eventually, I managed to scoop him into my hand.

I was being watched by a huge crowd who had gathered outside the shop's door. There were even some people inside the restaurant who had their faces squashed up against the window glass to get a better view.

Over the next few days, Russell became more and more disobedient, even though I had long talks with him. I explained that if he ran away, he wouldn't have anyone to talk to or a warm place to sleep.

Surely he could see that he was better off with me?

One day, he took a quick nip at my finger and jumped to the ground, scuttling away into some mud pans. I battled with some thorny cycads and slipped flat onto my back in the mud as I frantically tried to find him.

I searched for nearly an hour, but Russell was gone for good.

He'd gone back to his wild mouse ways. Somewhere in Tunisia today, Russell is probably telling some of our funny adventure tales to his field mouse friends.

It was wonderful to pedal my bike in this North African region – where some of the most famous movies ever were filmed, including my favourite movie, Gladiator, and also Star Wars! I continued my journey, feeling as strong as General Maximus Decimus Meridius and Luke Skywalker put together!

FLAG:

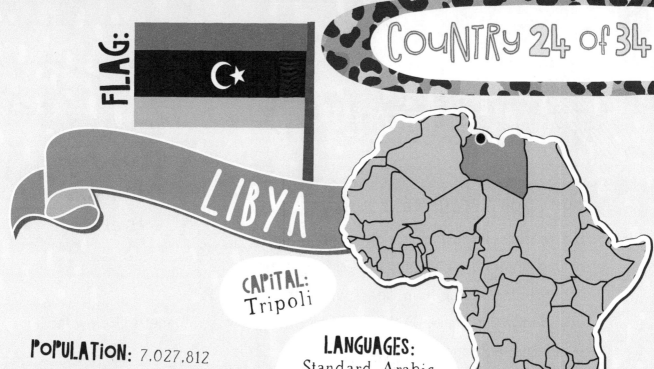

LIBYA

CAPITAL:
Tripoli

POPULATION: 7,027,812

LANGUAGES:
Standard Arabic (official), Libyan Arabic, Berber, Italian, English and others.

SPEAK:
'Greetings, how are you?'
LIBYAN ARABIC:
'Sabah al-kher, kif halak?'

CLIMATE:
Mediterranean (coast), desert(interior)

FABULOUS FOOD:
BAZIN
Barley flour is boiled and shaped into a dome, served with a meat stew and bean or lentil sauce.

ADVENTURE ATTRACTIONS:
Camel treks through the Akakus Mountains; dune surfing near the Ubari salt lakes.

FAMOUS PERSON:
ERATOSTHENES OF CYRENE
(an ancient Greek and Roman city close to present-day Shahat, Libya).
Mathematician, geographer, poet, astronomer and music theorist; he was the chief librarian at the Library of Alexander and invented the discipline of geography.

BORDER

TRIPOLI

ALONG THE TOP OF AFRICA

Imagine this: The world's first man-made river!

THE GREAT MAN-MADE RIVER is the world's largest irrigation system made of underground pipes and aqueducts, to bring underground water from deep within the desert to Libya's towns and cities. With four-metre-wide pipes, seven metres below the sand. A pipeline thousands of kilometres long!

In countries where there's almost NO water, ALL the time, this is what you've gotta do, guys. Already, one of Libya's major water sources is fresh water made from the Mediterranean Sea.

In Al Khums, I pedalled my dusty bike past the 2,000-year-old Roman city of Leptis Magna.

There, a group of bullies threw a bag of dates at me. It hit me so hard it almost smashed me off my bike. BUT FOOD IS FOOD!

And I found another smashed thing: a bashed-up phone on the road. It must have fallen out of a moving car. So I picked up the phone and kept the SIM card. Guess what? ⟶ Free airtime! Yeeha!

Meanwhile, underground, the earth rumbled. Because beneath the desert sand was 'BLACK GOLD': OIL!

Pumped out of the ground in dozens of oil refineries.

In the desert, I was so tired from cycling into the wind that I would tuck into my sleeping bag, and fall dead asleep. Until I was sniffed out by... desert hyenas.

SCARY!

Hyenas, you know, can crush a person with their strong jaws. So I made 'hyena burglar bars' out of crisscrossed spare

bicycle spokes, held together by a bicycle tube. I also pee'd around my sleeping bag area. To show them: "This is MY territory, you hyenas!"

Back on the desert roads, I would ask every car that passed for water – this kept me alive on my long trek through the desert. I would take a sip and swirl each mouthful around my mouth many times before swallowing. Next time you waste a single drop of water, think of how precious every drop is. Maybe, one day, you'll ride around Africa too – and you'll be prepared.

One night, in Sirte, near the birthplace of Muammar Gaddafi, I found a tiny TV showing a documentary about Nelson Mandela. When the people realised I was a South African, they danced with me in excitement. They thought I must be Madiba's friend!

Check the back cover of this book – you will see Madiba and me together!

But soon I was caught in a desert storm. Black clouds dropped tons of violent rain, like it was raining bricks. I crawled under a tarpaulin on the roadside, me and my bike huddling together.

One day, I came upon a terribly sad sight. Eight little puppies in the desert. They were just 14 days old, and desperate for water. I needed my own water badly.

But my dog-lover's heart took over. I just couldn't leave them. So I shared my last 300ml of water. They lapped it up with such happy little doggy faces. However, I couldn't take them with me on my bicycle.

There was one thing I could do: ⟶ Build them a little safe home. I found old planks and a piece of plastic and built them a tiny kennel. I felt so pleased to have protected my little adopted kids!

In Tobruk, I wolfed down deep-fried sandwiches, like the Cape Malay samosas back home in Cape Town, filled with delicious meat, eggs, vegetables and cheese. With a full belly, I was as excited as a man can be: in my next country, I was going to see the pyramids!

FLAG:

EGYPT

POPULATION: 105,604,242

CAPITAL:
Cairo

NATIONAL ANIMAL:
Steppe eagle

SPEAK:
'Greetings,
how are you?'
EGYPTIAN ARABIC:
'Sabāh elxir, izzayy
ilaāwāl?'

LANGUAGES:
Modern Standard
Arabic (official),
Egyptian Arabic,
Sa'idi Arabic,
Sudanese Arabic
and others.

FAMOUS PERSON:
CLEOPATRA VII PHILOPATOR
The last active ruler of the
Ptolemaic Kingdom of Egypt,
before it became a province of
the Roman Empire; she spoke
many languages and was a scholar
of mathematics, philosophy
and astronomy.

ADVENTURE ATTRACTIONS:
Horseback riding at the
Great Pyramids of Giza
and the Sphinx, Cairo;
cruising the Nile River
and going on an expedition
through the Valley of the
Kings and the Valley
of the Queens,
Luxor.

FABULOUS FOOD:
KOSHARI
Rice, pasta,
lentils and chickpeas,
topped with fried
onions and a spicy
tomato sauce.

BORDER

EL ALAMEIN

INTO THE ANCIENT WORLD!

At last, my dream was about to come true!

I was just 30 years old. But these mighty triangles were 4,500 years old! Ever since I was a kid, I had dreamed about seeing these with my OWN EYES.

✳ Manser of Africa was entering the land of the Pharaohs. ←

First, I pedalled my bike past El Alamein, a famous battleground in the Second World War.

Here, my friend Murray Williams' grandpa took a bullet to the heart. But he was saved by a thick little Bible in his breast pocket.

This was where British Field Marshal Bernard Montgomery beat the German Field Marshal Erwin Rommel.

On I rode to Cairo, one of the most populated cities in Africa!

And then, to the pyramids. I couldn't believe what I was seeing. Did aliens build them? It certainly looked like it. The maths and engineering were so brilliant, it looked as if computers had designed them. A hotel room in Cairo gave me a view of Khufu's pyramid - THE GREAT PYRAMID OF GIZA - 230m long on each side (with only a 0.1% difference in length between sides).

Those Ancient Egyptians were geniuses. Imagine what marks they'd have got at school!

I had now cycled up the entire western and northern sides of Africa – it was time to turn right, for the ride down the east coast, towards home!

Next, I sailed up the Nile in a graceful felucca boat. A lip-smacking meal on a five-star floating restaurant on the Nile made up for all the disgusting meals I'd had so far.

CAIRO

Before setting off again, I was given a gift: a new pair of cycling shoes. It was sad to say goodbye to my old ones, that had lasted me 21,000km through some of the toughest places on earth.

WHAT TREATS I GOT TOO: a bag full of South African favourites - like Liquorice Allsorts, ProNutro, Jungle Oats and Game energy sachets. Shoprite Checkers gave me so much food for my journey ahead that my whole back wheel broke from the weight! SHOT, GUYS!

In a place called Port Said, I got to see the Suez Canal. Check the map - it's where humans cut a MASSIVE canal out of the desert to allow ships to take a shortcut from Asia to the Mediterranean Sea. If it weren't for this canal, they would have to sail all the way down to Cape Town. Soon I was back in the desert.

SUEZ

I almost fell off my bike with shock when I set up camp next to a little bush, that turned out to be a swarm of screeching locusts.

THE BUSHES WERE ALIVE!

They crawled all over me, some even clinging to my face.

This is where I learned to first throw stones at desert bushes, to make sure they were actually bushes – and not stormy clouds of angry little marauders.

Further down the coast of Egypt, I was treated like a VIP, and given the 'FREEDOM OF SAFAGA', and the entire Red Sea region, by a famous army general, Saad Aburrida. That means I'm almost like the mayor there, for the rest of my life!

The general rewarded me for my incredible journey with a free ticket on a ferry to the Red Sea.

On the boat, the sea was rough, and all the passengers with me started vomiting EVERYWHERE on the boat. It was seriously disgusting. I stuffed napkins into my nose and ears to keep out the sounds and the smells.

But it was worth it!

The Red Sea is a diver's paradise, as clear as a swimming pool - filled with colourful hordes of eels and angelfish.

Back on the African continent, I saw so many wondrous things. Dancers who spin so fast, they're like dust storms. And the biggest camel market at Shalatin, where I gobbled up a camel steak too - a bit like lamb. I had earned it!

Soon I was able to rest, on a sailboat back down the Nile.

There, I saw one of the best sunrise views in Africa. It was at the temple of Abu Simbel, one of the wonders of the ancient world.

I saw, for myself, the rising sun turning the temple to gold, as well as the enormous statues guarding it.

Maybe you will see the same sight too one day?

SHALATIN

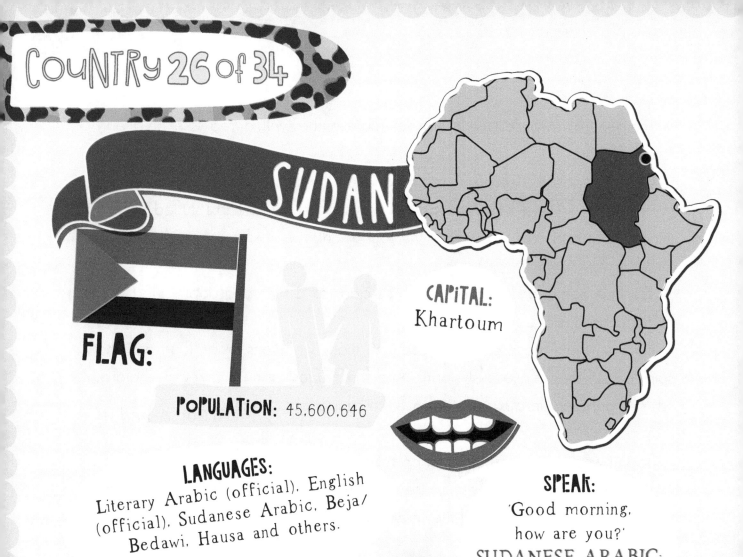

SUDAN

FLAG:

POPULATION: 45,600,646

CAPITAL:
Khartoum

LANGUAGES:
Literary Arabic (official), English (official), Sudanese Arabic, Beja/Bedawi, Hausa and others.

SPEAK:
'Good morning, how are you?'
SUDANESE ARABIC:
'Sabāh alkhēr, kēfinnak?'

 **CLIMATE:**
Tropical, desert zones

 CURRENCY:
Sudanese pound

ADVENTURE ATTRACTIONS:
Explore inside the Pyramids of Meroë in Eastern Sudan. Visit Souk Moowaileh in Omdurman City, the largest market in the country.

FABULOUS FOOD:
FUL MEDAMES
Cooked fava beans served with boiled eggs, vegetable oil, cumin, parsley, garlic, onion, lemon juice, chilli peppers and other vegetables.

 BORDER

 PORT SUDAN

LIKE A CAT WITH NINE LIVES

It looked like a train from the outside. But inside... man, oh man!

The train had no seats, no doors, no glass in the window frames. This must be the worst train in Africa.

And as it screeched through the desert, more dust blew in than air. I was choking half to death! Luckily, a Japanese woman gave me a surgical mask to keep out the billowing dust from my lungs. One of the other passengers died – and the train stopped for a few hours, so that he could be buried... SCARY STUFF.

This, my friends, was the Country of Dust.

And Khartoum was The City of Dust.

> If you REALLY love dust, this is the place for you!

Believe it or not, this is where the two Nile Rivers meet – the Blue Nile and the White Nile. The White Nile begins at the great lakes on the Equator, and is rich in light grey sediments, giving it a whitish colour. And the Blue Nile starts in the highlands of Ethiopia and Eritrea, picking up blackish-blue sediment on its travels. Together, they form the world's longest river.

In this land of dust and rivers, I met a Japanese couple, one on a racing bike. That was weird! The Japanese lady, Sakurako, kept on teasing me – 'cos I kept on getting lost in this City of Dust.

'You go so far, so long, around all of Africa, by yourself – and now you get lost every day!' She was right. The place was like a maze!

But oh boy, the food was DELISH! Fava beans with olive oil, tomatoes, onions, chillies and grated eggs, sprinkled with goat's cheese – a mixture mashed with an old Coke bottle and served with hunks of dry bread.

We were all so hungry that we used the 'wide-open-mouth' eating technique – squishing, slapping, and slobbering our dinner away!

Before I left, they made me scoop up and drink a handful of brown river water: there's a Sudanese saying:

IF YOU DRINK FROM THE NILE YOU WILL ALWAYS RETURN TO IT...

In the Nubian desert, sleeping was dangerous. I slept among scorpion-infested volcanic rocks. The local men wore swords to protect themselves against hyenas and desert lions.

One day, I had to leave the road, because the sand was too soft to ride.

I didn't notice how far I had ridden from the road, and then I realised: I was lost in the desert.

And I was running out of water...

I was like a cat that's used up all nine lives.

I realised I was going to die... and I said my final prayers.

But then I heard a rumble... a truck! The driver gave me water, a brownish-red colour, and it tasted like diesel.

But soon, another passing car gave me a bag of juicy mangoes.

Together, the filthy water and the fruit saved my life.

Maybe I was a cat with TEN lives!

NUBIAN DESERT

FLAG:

ERITREA

POPULATION: 3,628,684

SPEAK:
'Greetings,
how are you?'
TIGRINYA:
'Kemey hadirka,
kemey 'aleka?'

CAPITAL:
Asmara
(Asmera)

LANGUAGES:
Tigrinya, Arabic,
English, Tigre,
Kunama and
others.

NATIONAL ANIMAL:
Arabian camel
(dromedary)

FAMOUS PERSON:
DANIEL TEKLEHAIMANOT
GIRMAZION
Professional road racing cyclist,
currently riding for UCI Professional
Continental team
Cofidis.

ADVENTURE ATTRACTIONS:
Explore the junkyard
memorial of the Tank
Graveyard in Asmara,
dive the Dahlak
Archipelago from
licensed boats to view
marine life, shipwrecks
and pumice stones
formed by submarine
volcanoes.

FABULOUS FOOD:
ZIGNI
A meat stew spiced
with Berbere (a blend
of spices), usually
eaten with injera
flatbread.

BORDER

ASMARA

OH, THE AIR UP HERE!

It looked like a giant skateboard ramp. But it was actually an aeroplane runway – with a steep, upturned hill at the end. Just in case your plane STILL hadn't stopped...

> Welcome to the second highest capital city in Africa!

I landed in Asmara to get a visa, then went back to fetch my bike and cycle the same route I'd just flown.

Once, the Italians conquered this place, and it had a seriously beautiful Italian cathedral. Once I had trekked back to the Somalian border, and was back on my bike, danger lurked again. There were hyenas – numerous, nasty and noisy – outside my tent. They constantly woke me up, every night.

Fortunately, I soon came across the LONNNNNNNNGEST downhill in Africa, whizzing by villages where the local women had tribal cheek scars and large golden nose rings. Near the bottom, 15 men tried to steal my bike. I was ready to fight, because after travelling halfway around Africa, I was now tougher, stronger, leaner than ever. I had lost my sense of humour somewhere in the desert, and now I wasn't in the mood for them.

I was ready for one-against-15 – a whole rugby team of them! ←

> Luckily for them, a man in a Red Cross ambulance saved me.

FLAG: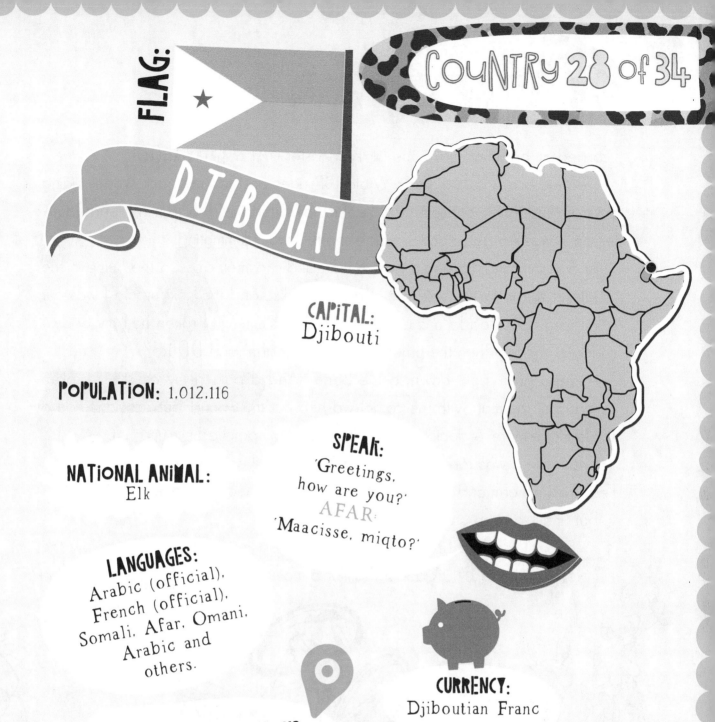

DJIBOUTI

CAPITAL:
Djibouti

POPULATION: 1,012,116

NATIONAL ANIMAL:
Elk

SPEAK:
'Greetings, how are you?'
AFAR:
'Maacisse, miqto?'

LANGUAGES:
Arabic (official),
French (official),
Somali, Afar, Omani,
Arabic and
others.

CURRENCY:
Djiboutian Franc

ADVENTURE ATTRACTIONS:
Dive and swim with whale sharks; visit the Ardoukoba fissure vents volcano near Lake Assal; drive through the Great Rift Valley to visit Lake Assal, one of the world's saltiest lakes.

FABULOUS FOOD:
SKOUDEHKARIS
A lamb and rice stew, spiced with Cardamom.

BORDER

DJIBOUTI

A MAN WITH A MISSION

I carried on barrelling down the hill. Fast, faster, YABBADABBADOO!

I leaned into a corner like a Moto GP rider and felt my back wheel sliding out from under me... but somehow kept my bike upright. I should have learned my lesson. It was like going down a mine shaft – I was plummeting!

At a slight bend, I bulleted past a man and a camel, crossed the hump in the middle of the road to avoid some jagged rocks... and the next minute I was out cold, lying on my back, in a cloud of dust. I was sure I'd broken half my body. I checked one leg. Then the other. Left arm, right arm — BLOOD!

A deep gash, right down to the bone... And a pain in my chest... a broken collarbone. The man with the camel washed out my wound. But I couldn't ride a single metre more. A doctor passing in an old 4x4 patched me up a bit.

Eventually, I was taken to a proper hospital, where they cut off some rotten flesh from my arm and dug out the dirt from deep near my bone. EINA!

But I had to keep on keeping on.

Soon, I reached Lake Assal, Africa's lowest point. I was 153m below the level of the sea. Think about that for a moment: → The sea was higher than the land!

SOMALIA

POPULATION: 16,659,362

CAPITAL:
Mogadishu

SPEAK:
'Greetings,
how are you?'
SOMALI:
'Subax wanaagsan, iksa
waran?'

LANGUAGES:
Somali (official),
Arabic (official),
English, Italian,
Bravanese, Kibajuni
and others.

NATIONAL ANIMAL:
Leopard

CURRENCY:
Somali Shilling

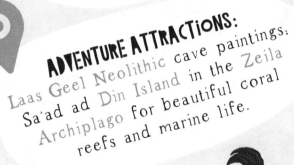

ADVENTURE ATTRACTIONS:
Laas Geel Neolithic cave paintings;
Sa'ad ad Din Island in the Zeila
Archiplago for beautiful coral
reefs and marine life.

FABULOUS FOOD:
LAHOH
A savoury flatbread,
eaten with stews
and soups.

BORDER

BERBERA

THE DAY I NEARLY CRACKED

A leafy green plant

I asked myself: 'Riaan, are you strong enough?' Ahead of me stretched another desert. I had 17 litres of water, two tins of sardines and two bags of fresh qat.

I needed to travel 60km a day, ride for 8–10 hours a day. Here goes...

I saw some strange sights:

A 102-year-old man running, hoping to set a new world record.

Another old man, a criminal, who was permanently chained to a large dog, as his 'prison guard'.

I WAS SUFFERING. Temperatures of over 50°C made walking impossible during the day. My trick was: dig a hole in the ground, under a thorn bush, and lie in it during the day. Then walk at night, until 03:00. But my mind was suffering the most. The intense loneliness, homesickness – I just wanted to go home...

My only companions were the sight of hundreds of camels in the distance, and old rusty Russian battle tanks.

My slog through the desert almost made me give up. But not quite!

FLAG:

ETHIOPIA

POPULATION: 119,850,133

LANGUAGES:
Amharic (official),
English, Oromo,
Somali, Tigrinya
and others.

CAPITAL:
Addis Ababa

SPEAK:
'Greetings,
how are you?'
AMHARIC
'Tadiyaas, indet
neh?'

FAMOUS PERSON:
KITAW EJIGU
Aerospace systems engineer,
space research scientist,
politician and visionary.

CURRENCY:
Ethiopian Birr

ADVENTURE ATTRACTIONS:
Danakil Depression, the lowest
point in Africa, to experience
active volcanoes, salted basins, hot
springs and a lava lake; the Simien
Mountains (God's Playground), a
UNESCO World Heritage Site,
home to the rare Gelada baboon,
Walia ibex and
Simien fox.

FABULOUS FOOD:
DORO WAT
Chicken stew spiced with
Berbere mix, which is
chilli peppers combined
with a variety of other
spices, like garlic, ginger
and fenugreek.
Hard-boiled eggs are
added towards the end
of the cooking
period.

BORDER

ADDIS ABABA

DIRTY DANCING

MUD, GLORIOUS MUD!

One minute I was riding through Ethiopia, then next minute I was caked head to toe in mud. All you could see were the whites of my eyes, like a spooky ghost.

A Land Cruiser rumbled up to help. With my bike in the back, we were full steam ahead. But the driver lost control. We spun around twice in the mud, like a ballerina. The 4x4 began to sink – soon, water was seeping in through the cracks in the doors. But the driver was brilliant, and the Toyota crawled safely out of the mud, just like a crocodile.

Further along my journey, I was so glad to apply my first-aid skills. A child had fallen off the back of a pick-up, or bakkie, as we call them back home. We got the kid off to hospital super-fast! That was a relief.

→ Be careful, all you kids out there! ←

I carried on, keeping myself going by munching on sugar cane – nature's energy bars. But when I wasn't concentrating, I ran into a herd of cattle and was charged and butted off my bike by a young bull.

Mr Moo stood over my bike and poked his nose into my bicycle bags.

The bull decided to charge again, but a herdsman came to my rescue, and beat it with such a vengeance, he almost beat me too!

Soon, I was in the mountain ranges of eastern Ethiopia: COFFEE COUNTRY!

I rode all night, sopping wet in the rain, to reach a village safely. And there I found the scariest toilet in all of Africa!

It was perched on a H-I-G-H cliff, leaning out, over the edge...

Was I going to fall to my death, just because I was bursting for a pee?

I ran off down the alley.

Eventually, I returned to face my fears, and managed to do my business without fear! I thought I should call this the www.theworldsgreatestspot2pee.com!

Next stop, a village called Hadar in the Awash Valley, where a famous female was found in 1974. They called her Lucy, and she was part of a skeleton of the hominin species Australopithecus afarensis.

HADAR

And Lucy was 3.2 million years old!

After all those deserts, Ethiopia was a blessing – was it the most fertile country in Africa? I passed fat cattle, with gleaming coats.

And it was in Addis Ababa, the capital, where I had the greatest surprise:

A VISIT FROM MY BEAUTIFUL GIRLFRIEND, VASTI!

Together, we travelled to one of the scariest shows in Africa: we fed hyenas, off sticks – just 10cm long, held in our teeth – with a piece of raw meat on the end. A hyena can crush a human skull with its powerful jaws. They lunged forward but, thankfully, took just the pieces of meat.

In Africa you find experiences like nowhere else on earth!

OVERCOMING OUR FEARS, TOGETHER:

After watching Vasti's face light up in Ethiopia when that hyena snatched the first piece of meat from the point of her stick, that she held in her teeth: Her excitement continued to buzz long after we were done, and I believed she was feeling the kind of energy that had helped me to survive during the more gruelling parts of my journey, and I was deeply grateful that I had had an opportunity to make this selfish journey of mine more memorable and real to her.

And it really did. The visit and encounter with the hyenas made her understand why I had left everything to do what most people thought was crazy, and in which she had loyally supported me, because she realised how important it was to me.

FLAG: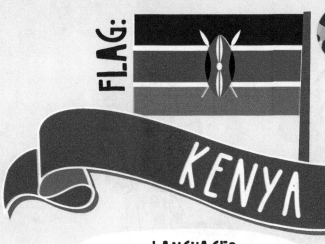

KENYA

LANGUAGES:
English (Official language),
Swahili/Kiswahili (Official
language), Kikuyu, Luhya
and others.

CAPITAL:
Nairobi

POPULATION: 55,791,646

SPEAK:
'Greetings,
how are you?'
SWAHILI/
KISWAHILI:
'Habari za
asubuhi,
habari yako?'

MOTTO:
'Harambee' (Swahili):
Let all of us pull
together.

CURRENCY:
Kenyan Shilling

ADVENTURE ATTRACTIONS:
Maasai Mara National
Reserve, for the Great Migration
of wildebeest, zebra and
Thompson's gazelle.
Amboseli National Park, for
views of Mount Kilimanjaro and
elephant and big cat viewing.
Ol Pejeta Conservancy, wildlife
viewing and chimpanzee
sanctuary.

FABULOUS FOOD:
NYAMA CHOMA
Braaied meat with salt
and pepper seasoning,
served with kachumbari
salad (tomatoes, onions,
green chillies, coriander,
lemon juice and salt) and
ugali (maize flour
cooked in boiling
water).

 BORDER

NAIROBI

SNOW AND MORE SNOW

I had travelled through 30 countries, 28,000km.

Now my body said "HELP!"

I was sick. Every bone in my body ached, my brain felt as if it was too big for my head. Was it a virus? What was wrong with me? I was scared.

A local sangoma (medicine man) gave me some lumpy, grainy, lukewarm 'magic treatment' liquid.

I can tell you, it was the most disgusting medicine in all of Africa.

I needed to get to a hospital fast – but there were no ambulances!

Instead, I caught a ride in a cattle truck and after two days, and 778km, I eventually reached Nairobi.

Soon, I was well enough for my highest challenge in Africa: climbing Kilimanjaro! I crossed the border into Tanzania, and my monster hike began.

With my new friend Jesse, from Canada, day 1 took us up to 2,700m.

On day 2, we went higher, up to 3,700m.

Day 3, even higher into the African sky, across a mountain desert – up to 4,700m.

Jesse was feeling weak, but I fed him full of popcorn and soup!

And on day 4, we began climbing at 01:30, for our final six-hour march, the last 1,250m.

But now we were walking on scree – tiny chips of volcanic rock ground finely by thousands of years of erosion.

It was like climbing a 1km-high sand dune. We took two steps forward and slid one step back. On Kilimanjaro, you have to take one step at a time. "POLE-POLE" ⟶ slowly-slowly.

After four hours, all we had left was a 200m climb. Now we walked on glaciers – frozen shelves of ice!

And at sunrise, we reached the Top of Africa – Uhuru Peak – 5,892m high!

At the highest point in Africa, it was cold: minus 13°C cold.

You can look down in every direction and see the whole puzzle that makes up Africa!

I nailed a small South African flag to the battered wooden frame.

Then I jumped 40cm into the air, as high as I could. So I got even higher than the highest peak in Africa!

Down at the bottom again, life wasn't so much fun. I soon had to eat the most GROSS meal of my whole journey: goat's brain and heart stew on rice. BLUAAGH!

I had to say to myself, over and over again: "HAKUNA MATATA, HAKUNA MATATA!" That means 'no problem' in Swahili.

This reminded me of my most delicious tastes of Africa, and my belief: "You can't always choose your food."

AND HERE IS A HARD-WON ADVENTURER'S TIP: Don't think about the source of the meat; concentrate on the taste, texture or smell, whichever is the most appealing to you. Part of life's adventure is to eat.

FLAG:

TANZANIA

LANGUAGES:
Swahili (official language),
English, Maaisai, Bemba,
Sakuma and others.

CAPITAL:
Dodoma

POPULATION: 62,677,847

SPEAK:
'How did you
wake up?'
SWAHILI/
KISWAHILI
'Ng'wa misha
gamhola?'

NATIONAL ANIMAL:
Masai giraffe

MOTTO:
Freedom and Unity

ADVENTURE ATTRACTIONS:
Witness the annual migration
of zebra and wildebeest in the
Serengeti National Park and
Nogorongoro Crater, climb
Mount Kilimanjaro, the highest
mountain in Africa.

FABULOUS FOOD:
MSHIKAKI
Beef kebabs marinated
in ginger, lemon and hot
peppers and braaied
over charcoal.

BORDER

DODGING HUNGRY HIPPOS

In Tanzania, I had my first taste of home: PAP 'N WORS AND BRAAI-BROODJIES!

But I wasn't ready for home yet.

I was in the land of the greatest mass movement of animals on earth – the migration of more than 2 million wildebeest, zebras and gazelles through the Serengeti and Masai Mara ecosystems, in search of greener pastures, watched over by the Masai – the famous warriors, with their spears and short swords, and their strange, stretched ear lobes.

South of Dar es Salaam, I set off on a ferry ride to see 12th-century Arab ruins on an island. And caught a mighty 12kg yellowtail for supper – the sashimi raw (fish dish) was delish!

Riding on, I reached the Ruvuma River – a magical place and one of the BEST camping sites in Africa.

At low tide, I caught a ride in a hollowed-out log, punted with a pole by the expert river man.

It certainly was wobbly – and he kept hitting his pole on the side of the boat, to warn the hippos and crocs to stay away!

I sat frozen, knowing that hippos kill more people in Africa than any other animal. If we came across a bad-tempered one, it would not think twice before biting the canoe in half, either mangling us in the process or feeding us to the crocodiles for lunch.

Was my trip going to end here, in a croc's stomach and with my valiant old bike gathering mud and reeds at the bottom of the Ruvuma River, like the Titanic on the ocean floor?

DAR ES SALAAM

At the southern tip of Tanzania, I felt as if the great baobabs, those iconic African trees, were waving a welcome to me as I pedalled along the beaten track that led to the border post.

Another country had been conquered on my own 'Great African Migration'!

MTWARA

MOZAMBIQUE

FLAG:

CAPITAL:
Maputo

POPULATION: 32,768,856

NATIONAL ANIMAL:
African elephant

SPEAK:
'Good morning,
how are you?'
MAKHUWA:
'Mocheleliwa,
ehali?'

LANGUAGES:
Portuguese (official),
Makhuwa, Tsonga, Sena,
Ndau and others.

FAMOUS PERSON:
GRAÇA MACHEL
Mozambican politician and
humanitarian; she is also the only
woman in history to have been the
first lady of two separate
republics, namely Mozambique
and South Africa.

ADVENTURE ATTRACTIONS:
Experience loggerhead and leatherback
turtle nesting expeditions at Ponta
Mamoli; snorkelling with whale
sharks in Tofo Bay.

FABULOUS FOOD:
MATAPA
Stewed cassava
leaves cooked with
ground peanuts,
garlic and coconut
milk.

BORDER

NAMPULA

NO MAN'S LAND

I entered a land so wild and there were almost no roads. Instead, only paths of thick sand. Sand so soft it was like trying to ride a bike through the sea.

So I had to walk – pushing my bike, slow as a tortoise. But in my path, I also had to dodge huge, steaming piles of...?

ELEPHANT POO!

I reckon only whales have bigger poos, in all the world!

QUELIMANE   CALE   BEIRA   VILANKULO

One enormous pile of poo looked fresh, so I stuck my left hand into it. It was warm! That meant elephants were probably nearby. OH DEAR...

So I scanned the forests of trees ahead – I didn't want to walk smack-bang into one mighty jumbo.

That was my big mistake. I was so busy looking UP that I forgot to check the road ahead. Until the last minute...

MY HEART RACED!

Across the road, right in front of me, was a 2m-long jungle python, stretched across the road like a bushveld speed bump!

I managed to stop just a foot-length away from her. She stared at me. I remained dead still. We were eyeball to eyeball. Like Mowgli and Kaa in The Jungle Book – remember?

Jeepers, I thought, those huge fangs are so close...

I almost wet my pants!

But, in the end, she slithered off into the thick bush and let me pass. What a magnificent serpent!

I was in my last country before home, and I had just met the wildest wildlife of all.

INHAMBANE   MAPUTO

FLAG:

SOUTH AFRICA

CAPITAL:
Cape Town (legislative),
Pretoria (administrative),
Bloemfontein (judicial)

POPULATION: 60,558,676

SPEAK:
'Hello, how are you?'
ISIZULU:
'Sawubona, kunjani?'

LANGUAGES:
Sesotho, Sepedi, Setswana,
siSwati, Tshivenda, Xitsonga,
Afrikaans, English, isiNdebele,
isiXhosa, isiZulu (all official)
and others.

FAMOUS PERSON:
NELSON ROLIHLAHLA
MANDELA
Anti-apartheid revolutionary,
political leader and
philanthropist.

ADVENTURE ATTRACTIONS:
Abseiling down Table Mountain,
Cape Town; bungee jumping
from the Bloukrans Bridge in
the Bloukrans River valley;
Kruger National Park to view
the Big Five - lions, leopards,
rhinos, elephants
and buffalos.

FABULOUS FOOD:
BOBOTIE
Spiced minced meat
baked with an egg-and-
milk savoury custard
topping.

NATIONAL ANIMAL:
Springbok

RICHARDS BAY

EAST, WEST, HOME IS BEST!

I was now almost the guy who had cycled around Africa. ALMOST!

Man, oh man, was it good to be home! And I didn't waste any time tucking into the best food in Africa: boerewors rolls!

I was now only 2,000km from Cape Town. But first I had to pay my respects to the town of my birth: Richards Bay. My gran, Uncle Jimmy, Auntie Su, my old school principal, the mayor - were all waiting for me on the City Hall steps.

My gran made the meal I always begged her to make - that traditional South African dish, bobotie, with its fluffy rice and wonderfully tasty, curried mince.

I had seconds and thirds!

Only 1,500km to home, then 1,000km... Summer rain fell as I passed Mtubatuba and Kwambonambi - two of the most beautiful place names in South Africa.

I drank in the rainwater falling on my homeland.

Next, into the breathtakingly beautiful Wild Coast, up the magnificent Mlengana Pass, to Coffee Bay, then Mvezo, the birthplace of Nelson Mandela. And past Qunu, where he grew up, near where Mr Mandela's umbilical cord is said to be buried, in accordance with traditional Xhosa culture - a symbolic linking to his ancestors.

Now just 500km to home...

The highest bridge bungee jump in the world is at the Bloukrans River Bridge. I knew that it would make great film footage, but I was very nervous to jump. I shuffled nearer and nearer to the edge of the huge bridge, with a thick elastic cord around my ankles.

The bridge was so high - I could only see air and rocks at the bottom. Big, jagged rocks!

YIKES!

DURBAN

EAST LONDON

I started to think about my journey and all the dangers that I'd already faced. This was nothing compared to those real dangers!

By the time I charged up to leap off the bridge, I wasn't afraid anymore.

Home drew nearer as I passed fields of sheep and ostriches. I realised again just how beautiful my country was.

On my left was the Indian Ocean, where the great rollers crashed onto long, pristine white beaches. Majestic mountains rose to my right. Now the kilometres were really flying past.

I could see the unmistakeable shape of Table Mountain in the distance – one of the most famous mountains on Planet Earth – welcoming me home.

My rugby club friends were there to cheer me on.

PORT ELIZABETH

Soon I was freewheeling down the pretty road to the Waterfront, where my journey had begun and would end.

I was going there to finish what I'd started, what everyone said couldn't be done. Vasti was there waiting for me, with all my friends and crowds of supporters.

When I arrived in the Waterfront, my ears were filled with so many voices cheering: "CONGRATULATIONS! CONGRATULATIONS!"

But what sounded loudest of all in my ears was the voice within me, that kept repeating: "Well done. Well done. Well done."

I was truly proud of myself. I was HOME.

CAPE TOWN

I hAd doNe iT!

BUT I REMEMBERED:

THE AMAZING THING ABOUT ADVENTURE IN OUR MODERN WORLD IS THAT THERE IS STILL SO MUCH TO DISCOVER.

Thanks for riding around Africa with me!
See you all on my next adventure!

AND REMEMBER, ALWAYS:

" FORTUNE REALLY DOES FAVOUR THE BRAVE, OR AT LEAST THOSE WILLING TO ACT BRAVELY. "

TRIP STATISTICS:

TOTAL DISTANCE COVERED:
About 36,500km by the map. The bicycle's odometer also tells us that I covered several thousand more during zigzags, backtracking and side excursions.

NUMBER OF TYRES USED UP:
About 120, the worst wear taking place on the tough roads of northern Kenya and Mozambique.

NUMBER OF CHAINS USED UP:
A total of 15. The first chain lasted 12,500km, all the way to Abidjan, but the replacement lasted only 10km. Ethiopia used up about 10 chains.

NUMBER OF INNER TUBES USED UP:
About 90 and some tubes having over 20 patches by the time they were discarded. There were far fewer punctures on the final leg, incidentally.

NUMBER OF COUNTRIES VISITED:
33, not including South Africa and the detour I made to Spain to avoid border problems in North Africa.

NUMBER OF BORDERS CROSSED: 35

NUMBER OF CYCLING DAYS:
About 808 days over two years, two months and 15 days.

AVERAGE DISTANCE COVERED PER CYCLING DAY:
About 90km.

LONGEST DISTANCE COVERED IN ONE CYCLING DAY:
215km in Morocco – thanks to a strong tailwind and the Western Sahara's very flat roads.

SHORTEST DISTANCE COVERED IN ONE CYCLING DAY:
25km at Oran, Algeria, after bumping into some fellow South Africans and staying over for the night (resulting in a very early start the next morning to catch up).

AVERAGE WEIGHT OF BICYCLE:
45kg, plus over 5kg of water (except in Mozambique, when dumping some items out.)

I've told you about MY adventure. Now it's YOUR turn to adventure! Start PLANNING your adventure below!

MY NEXT ADVENTURE